LAUREEN JORDAN

On My Eye

*What I Learned of Love & Life from a Syrian-Kurdish
Refugee*

First edition

This book was professionally typeset on Reedsy.
Find out more at reedsy.com

This novel is dedicated to my family, whose love and quiet support have allowed me to reach for the stars and live a life that I never could have imagined.

In memory of Kenneth L. Jordan
1944-2019

Contents

Foreword

This memoir is based on my memories and perceptions of events and discussions, and thus, any shortcomings are purely my own. I've changed the names of the people and some of the places (other than those in Istanbul) mentioned in the story. The quotes are not word for word, but paraphrases based on what I can recall. The English in the actual conversations was not perfect, but it didn't feel right to try to invent mistakes which might misrepresent the speakers.

Acknowledgement

This memoir, and many other stories, were made possible by the people in my life who never gave up on me.

Special thanks to my family for putting up with my time away and always giving me love and a home to come back to. Mom, you're my rock and my best friend. Thank you for believing in me. Dad, you were my safety net, always working hard to take care of our family. I miss you. April, since childhood, you have pushed me to be myself and to speak my own truth. Ember Lee, as a young woman, you've taught me what real courage is, but you'll always be my little munchkin! Graeme, you make me want to be a better person, and I'm so proud to be your auntie! Grandma, thank you for encouraging me to dream. I miss you. Grandpa, thank you for your strength and generosity. I love hearing your stories! Uncle Tom, you taught me the value of humor and kindness in life. Kyle, your focus on family is inspiring.

I also owe a huge thank you to my amazing friends! I'm lucky to have friends who are like family spread out across the world. I can feel your support no matter the distance! Thank you to the friends who have taken the time to read my writing and give me feedback and encouragement. You gave me the confidence to write and share this book! Thank you to my Latin dance friends. You bring me joy.

One final, and very important, thank you. Thank you to God,

who has shown me that life is magical and full of adventure, no matter where I find myself.

CHAPTER ONE

Freedom

Everything seemed just a little bit sweeter than I remembered. The sun was just a bit brighter, the colors in the flowers for sale outside Sariyer Çiçek were just a bit more vivid, and the air coming off the Bosphorous was just a touch more refreshing. It was a glorious sunny day on the outskirts of Istanbul, made all the more beautiful by the fact that I was on my first outing in months. Back surgery had left me locked up in my apartment, a prisoner far from home, dreaming of freedom from pain, boredom, and the same four walls.

I really shouldn't complain. Those four walls were quite cute, and that same apartment afforded me a window seat with a view of the Bosphorus Strait and the many ships and boats that traveled its waters. I could sit for hours on one of the wide windowsills watching the ships disappear and reappear from behind the buildings and treetops. Groceries and food from the many neighborhood restaurants were only a phone call or click away, and I had no shortage of friends visiting. Still, I had felt trapped. Trapped in my back brace, trapped in that cozy apartment, and trapped in my own head. But here I was, experiencing life again, and it had never felt sweeter.

I must admit, my imprisonment was of my own making. One second I was excitedly making my first Skype call from Turkey to the US to wish my mom a happy birthday. This may sound completely reasonable… until I tell you what else I was doing. With the exuberance of youth, or in this case, the folly of one who hasn't come to terms with her age nor her mortality, I was making this phone call while descending the steps from my loft in a pitch-black apartment. (I had been fighting with the Internet all day and hadn't bothered to turn the lights on when the sun went down.) One second I was happily contemplating how surprised my mom would be, and the next, I was in free fall, seeing my progress as if in slow motion, wondering if I would die when I hit the wall at the base of the steps. (I do, at times, lean toward the dramatic, but in this case, the concern was real. At the bottom of my stairs, you either went left to go to the kitchen or turned right to head into the living room. At this point, turning in either direction was beyond my control, and the blank, white wall was waiting below.)

*****

I didn't die. My flailing hand, by some miracle, took hold of a support beam on the way down. Unfortunately, momentum can't be so easily thwarted, and my body continued to twist, torturing my spine into an unnatural spiral.

Thus began a journey through pain toward healing, and ultimately to him. But first, the pain.

CHAPTER TWO

Strength

I don't think I really understood how serious my injury was at first. I took a lot of pain relievers and continued to go to work each day and teach through the pain. I told myself that it was just a strained muscle and that it would feel better soon. Truth be told, I was desperately clinging to denial.

You see, my dad had been dealing with not one, but three herniated discs, and the chronic back pain associated with them, for more than ten years. His doctors had told him that as long as he could walk, they wouldn't recommend having back surgery. They weren't sure that he would still be able to walk afterward. My dad's philosophy became: as long as I can ride my motorcycle, no one's touching my back!

So I grew up seeing the agony reflected in my dad's grimace nearly every day, watching him fold in on himself when it got especially difficult to move. He could no longer do a lot of the things that he loved, but he had a hard time accepting limitations. I watched him suffer, and I prayed that I would never have to face that same kind of misery. He's the strongest man I've ever known, often working double shifts through the pain to support his family, and I knew I didn't have his kind of strength. Now here I was, far from home, facing those fears head-on.

I tried to be strong like my dad, but one day it just got to be too much. We were testing our students to see if they had learned enough English to leave our program and begin their academic studies at the university. This entailed standing around watching the students to make sure everyone did their own work. We could walk around a bit to get a different perspective every once in a while, but too much movement would distract the students from their tests.

I stood there trying not to move too much, fighting to hold back my tears while shifting weight from one leg to the other in an effort to ease some of the discomfort. Sitting felt worse. Those were the longest two hours of my life (up to that point).

Later, as I walked home from the bus stop, I lost feeling in my right leg. Well, I should say I lost normal feeling in my leg. I could feel tingling as if it had been asleep.

Every story my dad had ever told me about dealing with his back issues came back to me. He often experienced a similar numbness. The fear was crushing, but there was no way of denying it any longer. It was time to visit the hospital.

It was a long, painful walk home that day, and an even longer road lay before me.

CHAPTER THREE

Facing Fears

T hat trip to the hospital was one of the hardest I've ever made. I was alone and in pain, but that wasn't the worst part. It's difficult to put one foot in front of another when you're headed somewhere you never wanted to go. Once I passed through those doors, I wouldn't be able to hide within my denial anymore. I slowly trudged toward the inevitable, feeling as if I was headed toward the guillotine.

When thinking of poor American me facing severe health issues far from home in Turkey, you may have imagined dirty hospitals with inadequate equipment and doctors who didn't speak English. The thought of being seriously injured in a foreign country where you don't speak the language sounds horrifying, even to me, and I lived it. The truth is that I was extremely fortunate. I was teaching ESL at a well-known university in Istanbul at the time, so my insurance allowed me to be treated at one of the leading hospitals in Turkey for a fraction of what I would have had to pay for the same care back home. It was a teaching hospital, so they had the best of the best to teach the next generation of Turkish doctors.

As I walked through the doors, I was impressed by what I

saw. The hospital surpassed any hospital I've had the "pleasure" of visiting in the States, which luckily haven't been many! It reminded me of a hotel. It was immaculate, spacious, and modern. The equipment was state of the art, and the staff was cheerful and able to speak English well, explaining the way to the Physical Therapy office, which would be the first stop in my journey.

My first doctor was a kind, intelligent, matter-of-fact physical therapy doctor. She was extremely knowledgeable, professional, and spoke better English than I did! (At one point, she gestured for me to get on the examination table to which I said, "Should I lay down here?" Her response was, "Yes, please *lie* down for me." I was properly schooled.) She ordered an MRI to see the extent of the damage and explained that I would have a team of doctors who looked over the results together to decide what the best treatment would be. My "team" was made up of my physical therapy doctor, a pain doctor, and a neurosurgeon or two. (And I was "lucky" enough to meet all of them over the course of my treatment). Their policy was to start with the least invasive treatments first, which I was happy to comply with. (I have an aversion to scalpels, needles, and all things painful.) After seeing my MRI, the doctors were shocked that I was actually upright, but since I was, we started with physical therapy.

I completed my physical therapy in the same department where famous professional soccer players receive their treatment. (Although I never got the chance to meet any of them in person! And believe me, I looked!) Twice a week, I would visit my physical therapists for massages, electrodes, and light exercises to ease the pain and strengthen the muscles in my back. I actually enjoyed my time there. I made friends with the therapists and melted under the warm, weighted compress, snuggling in to forget my worries for a while. As my back grew stronger, the pain and numbness began to subside.

Life seemed to be getting back on track.

CHAPTER FOUR

A Vicious Circle

A s my rounds of physical therapy came to an end, I started thinking about what I needed to do to build my strength and protect my back from future injury. I talked to some of my coworkers about how and where they kept fit. One suggestion was a gym in a well-known Istanbul mall. It entailed a 45-minute trip that included a *dolmuş* (a shared taxi ride) followed by a ride on the metro. Conveniently, the metro stop led straight into the mall, and there were plenty of other, more fun, places to visit while I was there. My friend recommended a Pilates teacher that she really liked, and I headed off to visit the gym.

Signing up left a bitter taste in my mouth. The facility was impressive, with all of the expected equipment, including a pool. Unfortunately, what I thought they were quoting in Turkish currency (*YTL*), they actually charged me in US dollars, which made it nearly twice what I thought I would be paying. Apparently, this gym was for people who had a lot of money or who REALLY liked going to the gym. I was neither, but I knew I had to do something to strengthen my back, so I signed on the dotted line and entered the vicious circle.

I started with beginner Pilates, and the first class was great! I went in a little early to talk to the teacher, and he waited patiently while I explained why I was there and what I had been going through with my back. During the class, he was constantly aware, warning me and giving me alternatives to any moves he thought might put too much strain on my back. I left that night feeling hopeful. Hopeful, that is, until I joined the Pilates class from Hades.

Everyone I had talked to had raved about her. She was quite popular and seemed nice enough as I explained my situation. It was just a beginner class. What could go wrong? Twenty minutes in, I was straining to complete a move with her laughter ringing in my ears. Looking around at all of the fit young ladies in the class, I should have known better. Just like I should have known better than to try to dial the phone while climbing down stairs in the dark. If I had not yet been introduced to my own mortality, it happened there in that Pilates class. I didn't realize at the time that the exercises I was doing were putting more pressure on my spine than it could handle, but I was soon to find out.

As I showered after the class, I felt something strange... then the pain slowly set in. I hobbled home that night frustrated and close to tears. In trying to strengthen my back so that I wouldn't re-injure it, I had done that exact thing. In my own defense, I didn't feel any pain or any physical warning while exercising, and at that point, not even my doctors were aware of the extent of the damage my original fall had had on my spine. But that insight came later, and in the moment I just felt angry, and frustrated, and really, really stupid.

CHAPTER FIVE

Doctor Pain

Enter the next doctor on my team. At the time, only in Turkey, and in Greece, could you find a 'pain doctor.' I know, because I looked it up. I felt so silly saying I was going to see the pain doctor! (Who am I kidding? I loved saying it! It sounded positively medieval!) The procedures that he performed were also done in other countries, but by various types of doctors instead of one doctor specializing in the relief of pain. After this latest Pilates fiasco, I came to know one well, but in Turkish, he was called Ağrı Doktoru. I found this term extremely amusing, when I wasn't in pain. He was to be the first, but unfortunately not the last, to perform a serious procedure on me.

He always had a joke (in English even!) and a smile for me, but I think he thought I was a little crazy. When he found me prepped for the procedure in my paper dress with my teddy bear clutched in my arms, he wasn't able to hide his distaste. I could almost see the thoughts pass through his mind… How many germs is this teddy bear carrying? How old is this lady, anyway? But then he looked into my eyes, and he must have seen some need there, because he allowed me this small comfort. (Actually, it wasn't a small comfort at all. Even if your doctors/surgeons and hospital give you the utmost confidence, it's still hard to face dangerous situations while far from home. Hugging my mom's teddy bear (the one I had begged and pleaded for, and probably stole, after giving my own version away with my heart years earlier) was the closest I could come to being with her.) You see, I am deathly afraid of needles, and the thought that would not leave my mind was that three very large needles were about to find their way into my spine. The first would remove some stuff (herniated disc to be precise), the next two would then inject other stuff (medicine to reduce inflammation and ozone to rebuild the disc). My worst nightmares were coming true!

My good friend and coworker, Janet, went with me to the hospital and kept me company as I lay there, fearing the worst. The tears started as soon as they wheeled me away, her promises to be there when I got out ringing in my ears. My pain doctor and the anesthesiologist didn't know what to do with me or my tears. Actually, they both looked so stricken, I thought they might join in! I tried to put them at ease with, "I'm sorry, I can't stop crying. I'm just scared. I don't like needles. Just do whatever you need to do."

At this point, I had a death grip on my teddy. In the moments before the anesthesia took me, my pain doctor reassured me that everything was going to be OK. He tucked my teddy bear under my arm and christened him with an honorary Turkish nickname.

"Puflduk will be right here when you wake up."

When I came out of sedation, I found that he had been true to his word. Puflduk had been tucked snuggly under my arm with care. Janet swears that I was speaking Turkish as I was waking up… telling people about my teddy bear. This was clearly a miracle because apart from a few key phrases, I can't speak the language. I have it from an expert (one of my students) that puflduk means soft. Actually, it was the pain doctor that turned out to be a big softie.

CHAPTER SIX

An Unfortunate Habit

O nce again, I convinced myself that I was well on the road to recovery until I encountered a hill that didn't agree with me.

In my defense, it was a cobblestone street with lots of uneven terrain. In the street's defense, I had walked it about a million times to get home from... well... anywhere. (OK, the million IS an exaggeration.)

Anyway, one minute my friend and I are almost to the bottom of the hill anticipating a nice, warm cappuccino from the hotel on the other side of the street. The next, I'm in free fall (again...this was becoming a habit) with my skirt flying up into the air.

Once again, it seemed that things were moving in slow motion. My foot turned slightly on the edge of a stone, and the rest of my body just went with it. I tried to muster the muscles that had always been there to keep me upright in the past, but there was no response.

I had time to implore Martie with frightened eyes, but she was too far away to do anything but look on helplessly. Her arms reached out for me and then lifted into the air as if to plead innocence.

I had time to think, "Oh God, I hope that guy in the convenience store doesn't see this! I have to go in there tomorrow, and he already thinks I'm crazy!"

Then I hit the pavement.

Luckily (for once), there were no cars intent on running me down in the middle of the street. Before you ask, yes, Turkish streets do, for the most part, have sidewalks, which is where I should have been. But the sidewalks that frame our adorable 17th-century road were frequently interrupted by gigantic steps that were unpassable for the average person.

Being considerably less than average in the maneuverability department, I found myself in the street. I didn't do a face plant or anything; My body just kind of collapsed down to the ground. As I gingerly tried out all of my moving parts, Martie offered me a hand. I was able to stand, but both me and my pride were badly bruised. Added to that, my back was already complaining about this rough treatment.

With the choice of a steep climb home or just a few more steps to the hotel, I decided to continue on toward that cup of coffee. I fear I wasn't the best of company with all of the worries that were preying on my mind. As for Martie, I think she spent the whole time fretting that I would pitch over again on the way back up.

CHAPTER SEVEN

Giving in

"Don't let them operate on you!" My dad's words kept ringing in my ears. The only problem was, I didn't have a choice.

We had tried all of the easier fixes with only temporary success. Each time I strained my back, the disc became more herniated, pushing on all of the nerves around it. My team at the hospital conferred, and I was told that I would be meeting the head neurosurgeon in person.

He was one of the top neurosurgeons in Turkey, and one of the kindest and funniest men I've ever met. He was assisted by a secondary surgeon and a wonderful nurse who was assigned to me because of her amazing English (and her limitless patience).

Truth be told, I think I fell a little bit in love with each of my doctors. Maybe it was my own vulnerability, or maybe it was the way they treated me like a human being, explaining things to me every step of the way, answering all of my questions, and offering me patience and understanding. I don't mean to brag, but I'm pretty sure they fell a little bit in love with me, too. They would light up when they saw me coming, and they always found ways to reassure me and make me smile, even through the dark times. Yes, I was set to receive an operation that I had feared my whole life, but I knew I couldn't have been in better hands.

During the surgery, they made a long incision down my lower back and went in to clean out the herniated part of the disc, which was putting pressure on the nerve. Everything went according to plan, and I was quickly trussed up in a back brace and sent home with strict instructions.

My friend Jonathan invited me to stay with him during the first part of my recovery. I quickly realized that even if I didn't intend to follow those instructions to the letter, Jonathan DID! I felt cocooned in love and support. Jonathan made sure I had everything I needed, and friends came to visit, bringing flowers and kind wishes. One friend even cleaned the wound for me since I couldn't comfortably reach it myself! This was all new, and to be honest, a little difficult for me. I was used to being the one to help others, and I've never been great at asking for or accepting help myself. Maybe this was the first step in learning a bit of humility through this experience.

I was touched by my friends' kindness and support, but it soon came time for them to go on their way and for me to return to my cute little apartment. The surgery took place at the beginning of the summer, so I gave up my month-long visit home to heal and get ready for the coming semester. It was a long, dull month, with everyone off enjoying their vacations and me trying not to do anything that may damage my back, again, which pretty much meant not doing *anything* I wanted to do. That's why I was so excited when the day arrived that I could finally go out for more than just a short walk!

CHAPTER EIGHT

At Last!

Now, after months of suffering the pain and boredom of being bedridden, the sun was finally shining down on me and my first day trip into Istanbul in months! As I mentioned, my apartment looked out over the sparkling waters of the Bosphorus Strait, not far from where it opens into the Black Sea. I lived in Büyükdere, Sarıyer, a distant suburb of Istanbul. To get into the actual city, I had to take a minibus, the metro, and then a bus to whichever part of the city I wanted to visit.

It may sound inconvenient, but I loved my neighborhood. The waters of the Bosphorus were my constant companion. They soothed me during my wait for the bus each morning, and then as we wove our way up the hill, the view of the strait would open up to display the two continents meeting in vivid blue water. I never tired of that view. Our university was built on protected land, so there was a lot of space and greenery all around. I've been lucky enough to teach in some fantastic locations during my career (some of them on a cruise ship!), and this was definitely one of the best.

Back in Büyükdere, our *lojman*, or faculty housing, still held the charm of the Greek school it once was but afforded all the luxuries of a modern apartment building. (Except an elevator, which would have been nice when doing laundry!) We had a large private yard filled with grass, trees, and a paved area for picnics and gatherings. As I mentioned before, it was a bit of a hike up the cobblestone street to get there, but it was well worth the effort to live in this hidden jewel of a neighborhood.

Our location on the outskirts allowed for a more traditional lifestyle. Many of the shop owners had come from other, more conservative parts of Turkey. Perhaps that's why they welcomed me with humble formality. The Turkish mom who made my favorite *mantı* (Turkish ravioli)by hand would always flash me a shy smile from behind her English speaking children. The baker down the street would greet me with a huge smile as soon as I stepped in the door and tell me what was best that day. In return, I would practice my hard-earned phrases of Turkish on him.

Büyükdere also allowed me to remain outside of this city that held around 17 million people unless I had good reason to go in. (This was incredibly convenient during the infamous Gezi Park protests, which gave my mother fits. As she watched in-depth news coverage in the US, I was far from the action and saw only a film about penguins marching like the rest of Turkey.)

Actually, I did see some of the aftermath of the worst day of the Gezi Park protests, and it was my mom's fault! Her best friend from high school was visiting Istanbul, and I had never had the chance to meet her. She had featured prominently in my mom's tales of her youth, so I made the trip in to see her. The regular buses and group taxis were being held up, so I waved down a cab. Many of the streets were blockaded, and tear gas hung in the air throughout the neighborhood. At

18

first, my driver was full of confidence, but the more we saw, the deeper his frown set in. I was beginning to doubt the wisdom of this journey. (Truth be told, I was afraid he would pull over any moment and order me out of the car!) With a little creativity, and a harrowed look on his face, he managed to get me to my destination. I had a lovely time with my mom's friend and her partner, and when I exited the doors hours later, everything was back to normal.

On this occasion, however, I planned to go into the old city to buy beads so I could spend my downtime making gifts for the friends who had helped me after my surgery. I also had plans to have dinner with an old friend who had studied at my university in the States while I was out. All of this would mean an additional tram ride that would add another hour or more to the 45-minute commute. You may be thinking, isn't this a bit ambitious for your first outing? And the sane answer would be yes. But I'm not a great patient (just ask the friends that helped take care of me), and I justified it with the fact that I would be sitting down most of the time. That, and I was strapped into a corset-like torture device of a back brace that would not allow any funny business, or natural movement for that matter. What could go wrong? (You may notice a pattern here...)

With that thought in mind, I flagged down a *dolmuş* and settled in for my trip into old Istanbul.

CHAPTER NINE

The Bazaar Quarter

As always, the history and beauty of this place struck me as I walked the cobblestone streets in the shadows of some of the most impressive mosques in the world. I had been told to look for bead shops near the Spice Bazaar, but I wasn't sure exactly where they were. I wandered through the winding streets, enjoying the savory aroma of döner kebab and the Turkish music filling the air. My vision was filled with the sight of intricate Turkish rugs, colorful glass lamps, and other exotic collectibles hanging outside the many shops. A window display of vibrant scarves and silver and semi-precious stone necklaces caught my attention. I had found the first stop in my quest.

The handsome shop owner smiled as he greeted me, and after a bit of browsing and conversation, he offered me something to drink. (This is generally the cue to make my escape. As a visitor to Istanbul, it doesn't take long to learn to beware the carpet salesman offering *çay*. It's difficult to refuse anything in the face of such hospitality, and the salesmen know it. One minute you're sipping tea, and the next you're walking out with a carpet that you had no intention of buying. But in this case, I got the sense that he was more interested in me than he was in making a sale.) Soon, we were sharing stories of our childhoods and who we'd become. His name was Ahmad, and to my surprise, I learned that he was Syrian, not Turkish. Each of his necklaces was a hand-made work of art. He had learned to design, carve, and cast original silver beads from his father as a boy. A few years before, he had come to Turkey, fleeing the war in Syria, and was trying to make a living from his jewelry in Istanbul.

We talked for a long while, and then he asked an employee to watch the shop so he could accompany me to the bead stores. I told him that he could just give me directions, but he wouldn't hear of it. He even stayed and talked with me as I looked around, which was sort of sweet and distracting at the same time. When I finally told him that I needed to meet my friends for dinner, Ahmad gave me his business card and begged me to be in touch. I left him with a smile and a promise to contact him. Then I headed to what was soon to become one of my favorite places in Istanbul.

To find Mimar Sinan Teras Cafe, one must look up. It's nestled on an open rooftop just across the street from one of the most impressive mosques in Istanbul. Süleymaniye Mosque, the second largest mosque in Istanbul, was built by Turkey's most famous (if my friend is to be believed) architect, Mimar Sinan, for Sultan Süleyman. It's large domes and decorative minarets make up a memorable part of Istanbul's iconic skyline.

I was a bit underwhelmed as my friend guided me through the entrance to a deserted floor in need of… well, anything. After climbing three stories, we were rewarded with an open area filled with people, laughter, and the faint fruity smell of smoke from a nargile carried on the breeze. Some people were sharing meals while others sipped tea and played backgammon, all within the shadow of the mosque's turrets and domes. We were so close, I felt tiny next to this wondrous architecture. It was as if I could reach out and touch all of that history. The only thing that could distract me from this sensation was the view on the other side of the rooftop. Here, old Istanbul was laid out as far as I could see in either direction. Its famous waterway and bridges were reaching for the Golden Horn on one side and making their way toward the Black Sea in the opposite direction.

*****

I guess I should warn you here that I'm a bit particular... In addition to seeing and hearing, I sometimes feel the people and places around me. Sometimes it's an uneasiness, a raising of the hair on the backs of my arms, that warns me to stay away. Other times I can feel the energy of the place and the people who spent time there. In these cases, it's as if I could close my eyes on one moment only to open them to find myself in another time surrounded by the people of a different era. It may sound strange, but the really strange thing is that, for a good part of my life, I thought everyone experienced life this way! (You can imagine some of the misunderstandings that might lead to!) Sitting on that rooftop, looking out over this vibrant city that I never imagined that I would see, I felt the beauty and the history as a physical weight. And my heart expanded with love.

*****

We sat for hours through dinner and then dessert and tea as

we reminisced. Truth be told, I never wanted to leave. It got even more difficult to imagine tearing myself away once the sun went down and the lights of the city and its bridges added their romance to the scene. Galata Tower winked at me in the distance as I tried to etch this beautiful view into my memory.

All moments must pass, and this one was no different. On my way out of the restaurant that night, I picked up one of their business cards and added it to Ahmad's card in my back pocket in hopes of returning soon. I keep that card in my wallet to this day, but not necessarily for the reason you might think.

CHAPTER TEN

Facebook as Fate?

I must admit, I was a little giddy as I made my way home that night. I had spent the evening basking in friendship, my own freedom, the beauty of old Istanbul, and the attention of a handsome stranger. After months of isolation, it felt like heaven, and I couldn't wait to reach out to my new Syrian friend.

Once home, I pulled the cards out of my back pocket and headed for the computer. There was the card from the cafe, my ATM card, and...well, nothing. No business card for the jewelry store! How could I have lost JUST his card? I thought back to my trip and remembered getting money out at the ATM in the metro station. I must have dropped his card when I pulled the others out! How was I going to keep my promise when I had lost all of his information?

The heart that had been soaring promptly dropped to the ground, and all of my hope went with it. But just maybe I could find him again... I typed everything that I could remember about him into the Facebook search...Ahmad, Syria, Istanbul. It was definitely a long shot, but it was worth a try. To my surprise, a list of pictures and names filled my screen, and I was faced with a different dilemma entirely.

I scrolled...and scrolled, looking for a picture that might resemble the face I had been thinking about all evening. I came across a pair of intense eyes and a dimpled cheek that were just a bit too attractive. It could be him, right? (In your dreams, Laureen!) Before I could lose my nerve, I concocted a witty intro, "Hi," and hit send. If it was my Ahmad, he would remember me. And if it wasn't, he'd just ignore the crazy woman.

Meanwhile, the crazy woman kept scrolling, and to my horror, I found my Ahmad. I wrote him a proper message and sent a friend request, all the while thinking about that "Hi" that I had left hanging out there for a stranger. It was echoing through my mind as I closed my eyes to sleep.

The next morning, I was happy to see that I had received a message. My jeweler must have gotten my message!

"Hi. How are you?"

Oh dear God, it wasn't my Ahmad. It was the guy who, if I'm honest and if the pictures were real, was so good-looking that I would never have been able to talk to him in person! And he was online.

"I'm fine. :) How are you?"

"Good. Where are you from?"

It went on like that, the typical 'getting to know you' questions until I couldn't take it anymore.

"Aren't you wondering why I messaged you?"

"No, I just thought maybe we had a friend in common."

From there, I told him the whole story. Instead of saying good-bye and wishing me luck, he just kept chatting. We chatted about work, school, relationships, and even my upcoming visit to the dentist. He seemed completely guileless and open. In fact, I saw an image of his dental x-ray before I ever saw his face. (In-person that is.) Our chatting went on for minutes... hours... days; until we finally decided to meet in person, all the while without a word from Ahmad the jeweler.

At some point, I put losing Ahmad's business card down to fate. I could just imagine it slipping from my fingers as I pulled out my ATM card, carried on a breeze to disappear down a grate somewhere and force the inevitable. (Actually, I'm sure it fell straight to the ground while I walked on as an oblivious fool.) In my heart, I know that I was meant to lose that card. I was meant to send a message to a complete stranger. I never would have thought that Facebook could be a vehicle of fate, but that day it was. Ahmed (notice the difference in spelling), who became MY Ahmed, didn't like to tell people how we met as if it made the story less special because it happened through Facebook. He preferred to tell the story of our first date. But me? Whatever you want to call it: fate, destiny, the Universe, God's hand... I'm open to it however and wherever it wants to show up!

CHAPTER ELEVEN

A Walk Among the Stars

I stiklal Street (*İstiklal Caddesi*) is the romantic setting that Ahmed preferred to recall when reminiscing about our beginnings. This cobblestone pedestrian street is lined with restaurants and shops, some carrying traditional Turkish products and others featuring international brands. In the evenings, a steady stream of people from all over the world flows up and down the cobblestones. They may be heading down toward the old city or up to Taksim Square, losing themselves in their shopping, or stopping for a bite to eat. Joining the flow, you're likely to hear snippets of conversations in various languages while taking in a wide variety of fashion, all against a backdrop of historic buildings boasting homes above and shops below. Grandiose buildings that used to house European embassies (now merely consulates) capture the eye and the imagination. Off of the main street, you can find just about anything you need, including rooftop bars that offer amazing views of the city below.

Ever practical, or perhaps afraid that I would be stood up and waste a trip, I arranged to meet Ahmed outside an electronics store that I needed to visit. I wanted to buy a backpack to distribute the weight of my laptop and books evenly to protect my back when I returned to work. I arrived early to look around the store and quickly found an acceptable, if not stylish, bag. I continued to look around the store as the minutes ticked by at an unnervingly slow pace. With all of my lingering, the cashier probably thought I was bent on shoplifting. Finally, the time was near, and not wanting to be late when I was mere feet from our meeting place, I paid for the pack and stepped out the door with thoughts of 'What if he's not here?' 'What if I can't find him?' repeating in my head.

I stepped through the glass doors into the gaze of one of the most handsome men I have ever seen. He was standing there looking up at me with a dimpled smile and intense green eyes. I needn't have worried that I wouldn't be able to find him. Even in that endless stream of people, I couldn't see anyone else.

"Laureen?"

His deep voice and warm accent made my name into something beautiful and exotic. I smiled, and nodded, and blushed like a damn fool. I hadn't even stepped down from the stairs of the shop yet! His smile widened (is that even possible?) and he moved closer. "I'm Ahmed. Can I carry that for you?" Flustered, I looked down at the forgotten bag hanging from my fingertips and struggled to find my voice.

"Sure! It's nice to meet you! Do you like coffee?" (I'm not very smooth in the best of times, and at the moment, I was incredibly nervous!)

We had set a meeting point but hadn't made any plans beyond

that. I had thought that maybe we could go to the Starbucks a couple of blocks down, but as we fell into step and slipped into conversation, I found I wasn't ready to arrive at our destination just yet.

"Is there a Syrian restaurant or coffee shop near here?"

"There's one on Çiçek Pasajı, but it's noisy. Do you want to go there?"

Noisy didn't sound appealing, so I decided to take him to one of my favorite places in Istanbul.

One of the most famous sights in Istanbul is Galata Tower. (You may remember its lights winking at me during our rooftop dinner.) It holds a special place in my heart because of its connection to early Italian immigrants in Constantinople. Just across the street from the base of the tower is a blue and white sign that brings back so many treasured memories for me: Lavazza.

Years earlier, I had lived in Turin, Italy for two years, and my favorite coffee bars were always those whose windows flashed 'Lavazza' in neon letters with pride. It was hard to find this brand of coffee in Istanbul, so it was always a special treat to sit with an Italian cappuccino in my hands and the bricks and lights of the tower filling my vision. But this time, they didn't fill my vision, but instead set the backdrop for an easy, if a bit too platonic, conversation.

"What are you going to order?"

"I don't know. I don't really drink coffee. I'll get what you get."

29

And so our relationship began, with him doing what I wanted because…well…because he knew I wanted to. It was too late to get up and walk away and find something that we would both enjoy, so cappuccino it was. Luckily, he liked it. (At least he said he did… I was later to find out that he much preferred tea.)

Conversation came easily, and we talked for hours of the past and the journeys that had brought us to this moment together here in Istanbul. He showed me a treasured 'American' Zippo lighter that he had been given as a gift. He told me of his hometown in Syria, just miles from Turkey. I told him of the small town in California where I grew up. He told me of his studies in Damascus, where he had gotten his degree in Computer Science. I told him of studying art and later teaching English in Italy and later on a cruise ship. He told me about his huge family, and I told him about my small one. I told him of my travels, and he told me of his job taking tourists around old Istanbul.

It was a pleasant conversation, but I was having a hard time reading him. I couldn't tell if this was just a friendly conversation or something more. He was very open and interested, but he was also extremely respectful. The cues that implied interest back home weren't there. He wasn't leaning toward me, and he hadn't touched my hand. And yet… My insecurities set in, reminding me that I was 10 years older than him and what someone kind might call 'curvy.' Meanwhile, he was smart, funny, and looked like his face should be plastered on one of the storefronts of Istiklal advertising cologne, not here in front of me sharing a cup of coffee and this conversation.

We left the coffee shop, but neither of us was ready to say good-bye. He took me to see a famous nightclub that my students were always talking about. Looking down at our casual clothes, we decided not to go in. Instead, we continued down Istiklal to a park on the Bosphorus. There were no benches available, so we sat down under a tree facing the lights reflecting off the water. By now, I thought he was interested in me since he kept coming up with new reasons for us to stay together. But I still wasn't sure. (FYI, I never am.) His shoulder was leaning against mine as we chatted. Did it mean something? As much as I wanted to find out, by this time we had been together for hours, and my back was starting to complain. (And the ground, all be it with a tree to lean against, was not the most comfortable place to sit.) But it was such a beautiful night under the stars and the lights of the park, and it felt so good in his company. I didn't want it to end.

"We should get back. The last metro will leave soon."

"Yeah, I should go," I said with a big sigh.

"I'm going with you... to make sure you're safe."

We climbed Istiklal together, with a little less conversation and a little more exertion. I was surprised to find that I was comfortable with him, even in silence.

I was busy turning thoughts over in my head. Did he want to accompany me all the way home? If we took the last metro, how would he get back? Did I want him to?

CHAPTER TWELVE

Firsts

I approached my front door with dread. I was happy to be there with Ahmed, but I knew what was behind that door, what I didn't want him to see. Dirty dishes filled the sink, my queen-sized mattress was on the floor in the living room, and who knew when I had last cleaned the bathroom? I hadn't had any visitors for weeks, and what I had been doing was wallowing in my own depression. My flaws and weaknesses were laid bare in that filthy apartment, and I was afraid they would disgust him.

I invited him into the apartment, and I watched for his reaction when he saw the mattress on the floor. Where I expected judgment, I just saw eyebrows raised in curiosity. I could almost hear him thinking, "How did she get this down here with her injured back?"

"It's been so hot, and the bed's upstairs where all of the heat goes. I wanted to be down by the windows."

I didn't tell him that I had moved it inch-by-inch by myself rather than being a bother and asking for help. (But from the look on his face, I'm pretty sure he guessed.) I had scooched, and pulled, and tilted, and scooched some more. Once I got it to the stairs, it was easier as gravity took over. The slippery tiles helped as well as I leaned it against different pieces of furniture on the way to the living room floor. I know now, and I knew then, that I could have hurt myself. But I tend to put others before myself (I didn't want anyone to have to make a special trip for me), and at the same time, I'm a stubborn Taurus. This would not be the first or the last time I put myself at risk to make things easier for others. (But I'm learning!)

"Do you want to move it back upstairs?" he asked.

Together, we returned the mattress to its rightful place, with me steering and him taking the bulk of the weight. Once that was done, I gave him the grand tour.

*****

"You're like a child!"

It may sound insulting, but it was said with wide eyes and a breathy voice. It sounded much like the comment "It's so big!" would sound when viewing the Grand Canyon for the first time. This came as he tried to keep up with me running around my apartment, telling him stories of the things I had collected there.

"My friends gave me this bamboo for good luck when I had surgery on my back." "My friend Jonathan found a collection of Turkish prints, so I bought a few from him." "This is where I do my work because I can look out and see the greenery and

33

the Bosphorus. And I hope to paint here," I said, pointing at the easel. "Oh, wait," and I dashed up the stairs to grab another treasure to show him while he stutter-stepped trying to decide if he was supposed to follow.

I tend to be a playful person. I was probably even more so that day because it was still the exciting, getting to know you stage of a new relationship. (And he hadn't been horrified by my lack of housekeeping!) Plus, I had been cooped up alone in my apartment for months. Truth be told, nerves also played a part. If I stopped moving around and incessantly talking, I would have to face the fact that I was alone in the room with someone who took my breath away. Without distractions, it would become impossible to flee his intense gaze. Finally, I ran out of things to say. My eyes dropped as he came closer. My heartbeat was racing, and my palms were sweaty. I felt him leaning toward me…

*****

From my description of him so far, you may be expecting a confident, sensual kiss. Hell, that's what I was expecting: a steamy kiss that would take me places I'd never been before. What I wasn't expecting was a soft, sweet kiss that was full of hesitation. Ahmed may have been a very attractive 30-year-old man, but he had also been sheltered by his surroundings, culture, and religion. He had only had one relationship (which was one more than was acceptable for a nice unmarried Muslim man), and it had been a long-distance one. He had only actually met her in person once, and that had been three years earlier. Ahmed had had very little experience with relationships and absolutely no experience dealing with a headstrong American.

At that moment, we began a dance of adaptation and acceptance. It wasn't always easy, but it opened up a new world for both of us. So in a way, that first kiss did take me places I'd never been before.

CHAPTER THIRTEEN

Charmed?

On the surface, Ahmed seemed to be living a charmed life. His job was to show people around some of the most beautiful sights in Istanbul, and the world. He spent his days among locations that had stolen my heart long before.

He led visitors beneath the iconic minarets and intricately painted domes of the city's famous mosques. Each one built to eclipse the one before, these huge mosques were designed to humble visitors in the presence of God. The massive domes and arches are covered in delicate repeating patterns of vibrant colors that combine to create overwhelming beauty. These murals are framed by rows of stained glass windows that paint the light as it shines through and illuminates the space.

Ahmed also led tours in my favorite place in Istanbul: Hagia Sophia (*Ayasofya*). Every time I visit this museum, which has changed her identity with the shifting tides of the city's history, I am overcome by the antiquity represented there. Originally a Greek Orthodox cathedral, it became a mosque under the Ottoman empire. I've always been struck by the coexistence of Christian and Muslim iconography. In a world where religions and cultures have sought to erase those coming before, here you can find frescoes of Janet and Jesus alongside the calligraphy of Islam.

Ahmed regularly walked the grounds of Topkapı Palace, the seat of the Ottoman sultans, and a place of revelation for me. (That revelation is another story, to be told another day.) Here, tourists can take pictures in the courtyard, visit many collections of antiquities, walk the path of the infamous Ottoman harem, and take in the view of the city from on high. The palace is also linked to one of the most mysterious sites in Istanbul: the underground Basilica Cistern. Amid the rows of columns individually lit by lamps the color of torchlight and the sounds of fish surfacing in the water below, Ahmed often explained how the builders had repurposed columns from different sites. Each column had its own story, none so intriguing as the hidden Medusa.

Ahmed's days were spent exploring Istanbul's history, and his nights were spent enjoying the city's modern nightlife. What could be better than that?

But is anything really as it seems on the surface?

As I got to know him, I learned that Ahmed was a refugee in Istanbul. Like the jeweler, Ahmed was Syrian, but he was also Kurdish. He had grown up just miles from Turkey but in a completely different country and situation. He had fled violence and lack of opportunity to find a new life, not only for himself, but also for the family he had left behind.

As a refugee in Turkey, he could legally be there, but he couldn't legally work to support himself. Working as a tour guide was one of the few jobs available to him, and his employers knew it. He was paid a low wage under the table. I would later learn that he didn't even make enough in a month to pay his rent. He was eating into his family's savings just to survive. As for his working hours, he had to be available whenever they needed him. It wasn't uncommon for him to work split shifts, taking a tourist around in the morning and then taking a businessman out to clubs at night. Being in this situation could take the shine off of any 'charmed life,' but it was better than what he had come from, and he was working toward something better.

This meant that I was a complication. In my experience, complications aren't kept around long, and truth be told, I'm not sure why Ahmed took the time to get to know me. He hadn't dated anyone in years because his focus was on the fate of his family. I don't know why he made an exception for me, but to Ahmed I became something more than just a complication.

CHAPTER FOURTEEN

Cherished

J
ust so you know, this is not the story of my first love. I've been blessed with several wonderful relationships, each unique in its own way. Ahmed fit into a pattern that I had of only becoming attached to people who were unavailable in some way.

Growing up, the example of love and marriage that I saw wasn't something that I wanted. What I saw looked like a prison, where trust is impossible because people change, and even the kindest of souls can be unappreciated. I've only recently learned to forgive, understanding that everyone is doing the best they can in any given moment, even me. Before that, I used to throw anger and blame around, and I resolved that I would never let anyone control me. I did try the traditional route to happiness once, but it ended with his fingers wrapped around my throat.

For someone like me, who feels so much yet trusts so little, temporary relationships offer solace. I can open up to the person in front of me without fear of what he might become because I wouldn't be there to see it happen. I can build illusions around what 'could be' if we 'really' love each other.

In the years leading up to Ahmed, it became more difficult

to create these delusions. I found myself wanting something real, rather than the relationships of convenience that I was offered. I desperately wanted kindness, respect, intelligence, passion, and appreciation, and I wanted it for a lifetime. But my subconscious wanted an expiration date.

*****

From our first date, Ahmed took every opportunity to show me that I was important to him. In Istanbul, relationships could be made or broken based on the neighborhoods you lived in. As you probably know, Istanbul is a city that spans two continents, and that can sometimes make it challenging to meet up with friends who live in different parts of the city.

Actually, that had happened to me when I had recently arrived in Istanbul. A dear friend, or perhaps something more, that I had met back in the States, and who had figured greatly in my decision to come and teach in Istanbul, couldn't manage to find the time to meet me due to the distance. (Part of that distance was the distance between parental expectations and the reality of who and what I was (American). Turkish mothers tend to want nice Turkish girls for their sons.) This also showed up with the original, jewelry-selling Ahmad. When I left that first evening, he made me promise to look him up and to come and visit him in his shop. There was no mention of him coming to see me.

Yet here was my Ahmed, working impossible hours for low pay because he really had no other choice, yet still making the two-hour trip to see me whenever he had a free moment. Not only that, but he felt fortunate to have the opportunity to do it!

"When things are bad at work, I just think about you and the next time I'll see you. You're what I look forward to."

What's a two-hour tram/subway/minibus ride compared to that?

CHAPTER FIFTEEN

What's in a Name?

A hmed didn't set out to teach me about Kurdish history and culture, but the stories of his childhood did a lot to illuminate a topic that I knew almost nothing about. Here I must warn you that these conversations have been filtered through my own recollection and understanding, or misunderstanding, of his words.

As I mentioned before, Ahmed had changed the spelling of his name on Facebook. The reason? Ahmed hated his name. Growing up, I had always liked my name. I was named after my mom's best friend, who snorted when she laughed, but the spelling was changed to be like my mom's. It's unique, beautiful (to me), and it reflects my family and my personal identity. I did have friends who went through stages of wanting to change their names, but it was generally to be different or to rebel. Ahmed's reasons broke my heart.

His family was part of a minority group (Kurdish) in Syria whose first language was banned in official circles and schools. Their family had a tradition of naming the girls with Kurdish names and their boys with Arabic names. Ahmed carried a name that reminded him of oppression.

More than that, up until a couple of years before I met him, Ahmed had had no official name. Neither he, nor his father before him, had been able to own property or obtain passports in their own names. His family's home and business had been purchased under his uncle's name. He had grown up within miles of the border between Turkey and Syria, but despite having Turkish grandparents on both sides, he had never been able to cross that border. My understanding was that at one point there was a census, but only some of the Kurdish people living in his city were officially recorded. As a result, as far as the government was concerned, Ahmed and his family did not officially exist. This left him powerless in a lot of ways, without the civil rights that I have taken for granted my entire life.

Another story from his childhood that challenged my own privilege involved the arrest of his father.

"The government could do whatever they wanted. When I was a boy, my father was in jail for a month for no reason. I had to search through all the papers and receipts from the pharmacy and prove that everything we were selling we got legally."

In this system, the responsibility fell on Ahmed, as the oldest son, to prove his father's innocence, rather than on the police to prove guilt. I can't imagine the pressure placed on him to free his father and re-open the family business so they could support themselves. I imagine he must have felt powerless and guilty for every day that his father was in jail. All of this, and he was still a child at the time!

As he told me of his childhood, there was never any anger in his voice. This was just how life had been for him. But I felt angry. I wanted to protect him, to take away every childhood hurt. But all I could do was love and accept him in that moment, and that's what I did.

Ahmed, and others like him, gained more rights during the war.

"They wanted to make us happy because they wanted help with the war. They made it so we could get our passports. As soon as I got mine, I came to Istanbul. I started as a student, studying at a [Turkish] language school. Then I changed my visa to refugee."

As I mentioned, while refugee status allowed him to stay in Turkey, it didn't allow him to make a living. At one point, his whole family (all 8 of them) came to live with him in Istanbul. His old roommates moved out so that they could move in. Unfortunately, he was the only one working, and he wasn't making enough to pay the rent, let alone food, utilities, and all of the things a family needs. It was an impossible situation, but Ahmed's family were among the lucky ones. While, like others, they had been forced to leave their home and business behind, they had some savings to live on. The problem was that those savings wouldn't last forever. They would have to find a solution, a way to start a new life. Being the oldest son, Ahmed's job was to find one, and this prospect hung over our relationship until its end.

CHAPTER SIXTEEN

Under My Umbrella

A hmed came to see me every chance he got, so we started to create our own traditions.

He accepted me exactly as I was, which not everyone in my life has done. If you were to ask someone close to me about me, they would probably soon mention my laugh or smile. (Almost every good-bye note that I've ever received from a student has been some version of "I'll miss your smile.") I laugh *a lot*, and it's made it difficult for me to get close to some people because they have the suspicion that I'm laughing *at* them. I laugh and joke around, and that joking is sometimes tinged with sarcasm. I've learned to tone it down over the years so as not to hurt people, but I tend to get closest to those who can handle a bit of sarcasm, who can let me be me. I could be myself with Ahmed, and even though it sometimes gave him pause, it was always greeted with a smile.

I can also be a very affectionate person. While this was perfectly fine and encouraged in private, it was awkward for him in public. The first time I took his hand as we walked along the Bosphorus, he drew away a little bit, and the emotion vanished from his face; but he didn't let go. I watched him from the corner of my eye, planning to let go if his discomfort continued. Instead, after a few steps, he relaxed, and a huge smile slowly spread across his face. That became one of his favorite things to do, and we would walk and dream and joke about how we would buy this or that houseboat and just sail away together.

Our first double date brought about new, new territory. I had invited my neighbor Josephine and her boyfriend to join us for dinner at a well-known chicken restaurant nearby. (People raved about the chicken wings, but it was the dessert that I was after!) It had been raining all day, so Ahmed grabbed his umbrella on the way out. Just outside the door, when he opened the umbrella and held it up for us, I instinctively tucked in under his arm and put my arm around him. I felt his body tense, but he didn't pull away. He soon relaxed, and we walked down the cobblestone street wrapped in each other's arms, sheltered under the umbrella, chatting about what to expect of my friend.

When we arrived, we found that Josephine's boyfriend had canceled, so it was just the three of us. Ahmed was a little quiet at first, but he was soon able to join the conversation, and we all shared a nice meal. At one point, I asked him for a towelette. Josephine and I watched him pick one up... open the packet... remove the towelette... and UNFOLD it before finally presenting it to me with a little flourish. After exchanging a quick glance and a raised eyebrow with Josephine, I accepted it with a blush, knowing that anyone else I had ever known would have just handed me the packet without a second thought or glance. But that was my Ahmed.

As we left the restaurant that night, Ahmed rushed to go out the door first. With a dashing smile, he turned and opened the umbrella (also with a flourish), raising his arm to usher me into my place at his side. We said our good-byes and snuggled in for our walk back up the cobblestones. He was getting the hang of public displays of affection, and from the look of it, he was enjoying himself!

CHAPTER SEVENTEEN

On My Eye

Over time, my happiness became Ahmed's happiness. He never showed up to my home empty-handed. The gifts weren't extravagant; he had very little money. (Which is why I felt guilty that he was doing all of this traveling to come and see me, but he wouldn't let me give him a dime.) The gift would be a bag of mandarin oranges, fresh peanuts from the open-air market, or a treat from the bakery down the street. I learned not to let my eyes linger on pretty things because I knew he would move heaven and earth to try to get them for me. I started to search for little things that I thought he would like. Two could play at this game!

One night we were getting ready for dinner, and I had forgotten the salt. Since he was standing in the kitchen, I called over to him,

"Can you do me a favor?"

He turned and looked at me, all solemn green eyes and serious expression.

"I'm ready to do anything for you."

*****

It's hard to explain how this felt, especially since I had never felt anything like it before going to Turkey. There was one other incident that gave me a similar feeling, and it was with my first class of Turkish students. These students had been labeled 'at risk' because they would be kicked out of the university if they weren't able to pass an English proficiency test at the end of the semester. To make matters worse, they knew that the school thought of them as at-risk, and many of them had already given up.

I'll never forget when one of them said to me, "You really believe in us, don't you?"

He sounded so surprised, and I was disappointed that he hadn't felt that before from previous teachers.

Fast forward to the end of the semester and our last day of class. We had brought snacks and were celebrating their success when one of them asked if he could kiss my hand. Flustered, I told him that wasn't necessary, but he explained that it was a way for them to show respect.

I said a doubtful OK, and then most of the boys formed a line in front of me. They took turns solemnly kneeling on one knee in front of me (I was standing) and lifting my hand to kiss the back of it. One student even kissed my hand and then brought it to the top of his head. I remember thinking that I now knew what the Pope feels like when people kiss his ring, but I kept my jokes to myself because it felt like they were giving me a precious gift, their utmost respect.

I later learned that this ceremony was usually for adults who were like honorary grandparents to kids. (That made it a little less flattering!) For my students, it was a way to show respect and thank me for all that I had done for them.

*****

When I heard Ahmed's declaration, it took my breath away.

He went on to explain, "We have a saying, 'On my eye.' When you... care about someone... you would do anything for that person. It means that if you asked, I would take out my eye and give it to. If you asked for my head, I would give you that, too."

Apparently, 'on my eye' is a common expression throughout the Middle East and Turkey, but I could see from the gravity in his eyes that Ahmed meant it with all his heart. It's a shame that I couldn't ask for what I really wanted, but it was the only thing I knew he couldn't give.

CHAPTER EIGHTEEN

Broken

Several months into our relationship, I opened my eyes on a bright, beautiful Saturday morning. As I stretched and moved toward the edge of the bed to get up, I noticed a little stiffness in my back and wondered why. I couldn't remember doing anything strenuous the day before. I sat up and put my feet on the floor, leaned forward to stand up, and immediately crumpled back onto the bed in pain. Until this moment, I didn't know what unbearable pain was. Now it was telling me that all of the physical therapy, pain-blocking procedures, and the surgery to clean up the herniated disc had all been for nothing. My back was done for.

I spent that day in bed rather than calling an ambulance or a taxi and heading straight to the hospital. It was the weekend after all, so my doctors wouldn't be there. And it's not like I didn't know what was wrong. I had grown up in a family that only went to the hospital if someone was near to death, and *never* on a weekend. But really, it probably came down to fear. And after all, it didn't hurt when I lay down. I decided to ride it out until Monday.

Ahmed's voice on the other end of the line was filled with

concern, but he was working a split shift that day, some hours in the morning, and then others later in the evening. I was on my own. Which wouldn't have been all that bad if I didn't need to eat or use the restroom. Unfortunately, I'm only human, and I would lie there with tears streaming down my face, knowing that my stomach and bladder wouldn't be able to hold out forever. Eventually, I would have to get on my feet and face that pain again.

When forced to move, I developed a strange golem-like gait, attempting to take the pressure off my spine while shuffling as quickly as I could to wherever I was headed so I could get off of my feet once more. The only thing I ate was oatmeal since it only took a minute to cook. I would throw everything in a bowl through my tears and then shuffle to the couch to lie down while the microwave whirred. Then I'd have to find the courage to stand and retrieve it and then return to the couch to lie on my side to eat. To make matters worse, my bedroom and bathroom were upstairs in the loft area, and the kitchen was downstairs. Oh, how I hated those damn stairs.

I passed a day and a night like this, and then on Sunday, he came to me with takeaway in his hand. He had called to tell me he was on his way, so I made my way downstairs to lie on the couch and wait. I hate to think of what I must have looked like... I had brushed my teeth through the tears, but I hadn't changed out of my pajamas, brushed my hair, or really looked into a mirror for days. I shuffled to the door at his knock, turned the knob to release the lock, and then shuffled quickly away and up the stairs to my bed, leaving his hurt "wait" behind. He was used to hugs and kisses at the door, but in this state, I couldn't even endure that. He followed me up the stairs, where I told him, "I'm sorry, it just hurts so bad." His eyes were glassy with tears as he climbed into bed and laid our meal out between us. After we finished eating, he held me in his arms as long as he could, but we both knew that he would have to go eventually. I promised him that I would go to the hospital first thing in the morning, and he promised me that he would come to find me as soon as he could.

The next day was quite easily the worst day of my life. Once dressed, I made my way (golem-like) down to the security booth at the main entrance to ask them to call a taxi to take me to the hospital. The guard got me a chair to sit in, but it hurt to bend my back into it, so I sat on the edge and leaned back, trying to keep my back straight. I would have done nearly anything to stop crying so that people would stop looking at me with such pity in their eyes. I felt like I was hurting them by displaying my pain so openly, but there was absolutely nothing I could do about it.

In the taxi, I laid back across the back seat, tears streaming, and watched the reflection of the driver's fear-filled eyes in the rear-view mirror. We flew along the Bosphorus, and I wondered if I was going to meet my end right there in that car before we even got to the hospital. He bobbed and weaved through traffic, hitting speeds I wouldn't have imagined possible on that stretch of road. Soon we were parked in front of the hospital entrance, both of us relieved that I was still alive. I threw some bills at the driver as I gingerly made my way out of the car. I didn't know exactly where to go, so I headed to the most familiar place in the hospital.

My physical therapist found me with tears streaming down my face, writhing in pain in a waiting room chair, and kindly invited me to lie down on one of the physical therapy beds while I waited for the doctor. That was the beginning of my being shuttled by wheelchair, which was torture, to my doctor, the ER (where they shot me up with pain medication that did nothing to ease the pain), Radiology (for my 3rd MRI in as many months), back to the physical therapy bed, back to my doctor, to the assistant neurosurgeon, to the senior neurosurgeon, and finally to in-patient services. The whole time I felt like I was on display, with people staring at my tears while I had no way of stopping them. Finally, blessedly, I was taken to a hospital bed.

My primary neurosurgeon rushed in with a, "Why didn't you come in sooner? We could have gotten the pain under control!"

My original injury had been accompanied by pain and an alarming numbness in my left leg. During his examination, he told me that I had lost strength in my big toe. (It sounds kind of funny now as I write those words, but at the time, it was scary to be unable to resist the pressure he was applying. It's a startling discovery to find that your body has betrayed you, even if it is just a big toe! He was pretty sure that I would need to have my spine fused, but they needed to take some x-rays first. And those couldn't be done until I could move without screaming.

CHAPTER NINETEEN

Pre-Op

I could see the fear in their eyes as they hesitantly approached the door of my hospital room. I imagine they roshamboed to see who got to visit me on their rounds, and I don't think I was a prize for the winner.

It's not that I was mean to the nurses, it's just that we had a hard time communicating. I only know a few words of Turkish, and most of them knew even less English, so we were reduced to an ongoing game of charades. It didn't help that I wasn't supposed to get out of bed without calling for help, so I called a LOT. If I needed to use the little girls' room, I had to call. Wanted to turn the lights out? Call. And point. And mime going to sleep. (It's amazing how many times that could be misinterpreted!) If the phone rang, oh just forget it! (Unless I was lucky enough to already be up.) Each time one of them entered the room, I could see him or her visibly take a deep breath and stand a little taller while screwing up the courage to take the bull by the horns, so to speak. I was the bull.

The best (or worst) part was the changing of the guard. Every morning at six o'clock, the hunky young male nurses of the night shift made way for the sweet young female nurses of the day shift, and they inexplicably converged on my room. The first morning was quite alarming. Feeling vulnerable in my tubes and hospital gown, I looked up at the knock on the door (which I swear I had heard at least once an hour since my arrival). I was shocked as nurse after nurse after nurse filed into the room. Once they had all piled in, eight of them at least, they all stared at me as if I may attack at any given moment, and I stared at them. And we kept staring. Finally, some brave soul said, "Hello." I replied, "Hello," to which they all nodded and filed back out of the room. I just stared after them, wondering what had just happened and what I was supposed to do about it.

CHAPTER TWENTY

Spider-Woman

O n my second day, once the drugs had sufficiently taken the pain away, I was wheeled through the hospital for 'dynamic' x-rays. To determine what kind of surgery I needed, they first had to see if there was an instability in my spine that was causing the recurring disc herniation. To do that, they had to take x-rays of my back in action. Sure, it sounds easy enough. It wasn't.

The process began with me lying on a cold, metal platform a couple feet off the ground. I was still in some pain, but the IV had done the trick, so this was doable, if a little uncomfortable. A few pictures were taken, and then the platform started to move. To understand, try to imagine yourself in the back of a dump truck that is trying very hard to remove you. One end of the platform was raised, and I didn't know whether to worry that I wouldn't be able to hang on or that there might not be anything under my feet. I was scrambling to stay on the contraption, feeling like Spider-Man out on a ledge, begging with my eyes to hold on to an arm of the machine above me. The technician grimly shook his head and pointed to the top of the wall I was now against, so I clung to that with all of my might.

Unfortunately, I didn't have much might. As the platform continued to incline, I went from Spider-Woman to just plain Laureen trying to stay on something that felt like a mechanical bull. I shot a guilty look at the technician as I touched that arm I wasn't supposed to touch. He was not impressed. Somehow, I found my balance on the plank I imagined under my feet, and I gave a wobbly smile in triumph. Still unimpressed, he motioned for me to turn to the side. At this point, I was ready to have a panic attack, that is until I looked down.

That "ledge" I was standing on was at least a foot and a half wide! I sheepishly smiled at him again, and finally, that stoic face broke into a grin. (I suspect that contrary to appearances, that man really does enjoy his job.) There was more twisting and turning involved, but by then, I knew I wasn't going to fall to my death, and if I did fall, I could easily step back up.

CHAPTER TWENTY-ONE

Preparing for Fusion

A fterward, I was returned to my nurses, who I slowly won over. (It might have been the teddy bear that won them over; it's difficult to be afraid of a bull with a teddy bear!) Soon they were fighting over who got to come to my room and practice their few words of English, of which 'pain' factored in a lot, but at least they were trying to get rid of it and not cause it!

You might be asking yourself if I was ever scared that I couldn't communicate with my nurses.

The answer is no, I wasn't scared. I wished my mom was there with me, but I knew I was being cared for by some of the best doctors in the country. My team of doctors and my primary nurse were quick to respond to any question or request I had at any time. (Which I took full advantage of.) My surgeons visited me twice a day, and my nurse was there three or four times. Unfortunately, the news that they brought after my x-rays was that I did have instability in my spine, so they would have to put screws into my back to stabilize it. Even worse, it was the lower portion of my spine that was being fused, so my range of motion would be affected. How much remained to be seen.

You may also be wondering about the accommodations in a Turkish hospital. Was it dirty? What was the food like? I had a huge room all to myself with a large picture window showing off the distant hillside with apartment buildings and a mosque or two silhouetted against the sky. My hospital bed was extremely comfortable, covered in warm blankets and adjustable to whatever position I might imagine I wanted to be in. (I wished I could take that bed home with me!) The place was pristine, and the food was better than what I cooked for myself at home. The people in the two countries that I've spent the most time in (outside of my own), Italy and Turkey, really value their food heritage. It follows that time spent in a hospital healing there would include meals that are as close to home-cooked as possible.

I was able to call and receive phone calls from home whenever the time difference would allow, so my family knew exactly what was going on, and I had them close to my heart the whole time. And so, I felt anything but alone when it came time for the surgery.

The last thing I remember before being wheeled through the hospital in my bed was hearing my doctor explain to the people that were getting me ready,

"She's very sweet, but…"

At that point, he walked out of the room, but I probably wouldn't have understood the Turkish anyway. I could imagine what came after that but: she's very sensitive, terrified, crazy, or all of the above and more. I pondered this during the trip to the OR, but I was asleep long before we arrived.

CHAPTER TWENTY-TWO

ICU

I woke up in a dimly lit room with more bruises and tubes attached to me than I could account for. The pillow, blankets, and guard rail formed a suffocating cocoon around me. All I could move/feel were my eyes, which made it difficult to assess the damage. My tongue felt swollen in my mouth as I struggled to bring some moisture to it. I was in a private room, but not the nice kind.

I was alone, surrounded by observation windows where one bored nurse watched me between chats with her friends, but I felt completely cut off. All I wanted at that moment was a sip of water and to be told that everything was OK. While I could see nurses rushing past down the hall and the one who stared at me from a chair by one window, no one seemed particularly interested in me. I looked around for a call button and found nothing. I was wedged into my bed with little chance of moving, much less escaping. My weak wave was ignored, as was my best imploring gaze. My ears were filled with the sounds of muffled Turkish. Eventually, my jailer got tired of me staring back at her and came in with a frown.

"Effendim?"

I sucked my tongue to build up the moisture to speak, "Can I please have some water?"

"Iglezce yok."

"Su, lutfen?"

The hand on her hip and purse in her lips told me that I was asking far too much, but she did bring a small cup of water with a straw. I had one second to get what I could before she stole the cup away, setting it on the windowsill across the room from me as she left without a backward glance.

He found me there, staring at that damn cup while mentally deriding Turkish hospitals and the cruel nurses who worked there. He had a harassed look on his face, quite close to tears, actually, but he looked like a guardian angel to me.

"I brought you flowers, but they wouldn't let me bring them to you!"

"That's OK. I'm glad you're here!"

"I took some pictures, see?"

"They're beautiful, thank you!" I couldn't move much, but I could manage a smile for him. "But honey, why do you look so sad?"

"They wouldn't let me bring them to you."

It made perfect sense, and if ever the saying "it's the thought that counts" was true, it was in that moment. I knew that Ahmed didn't earn enough money to buy what he needed, let alone buy me flowers that he couldn't even give me. I never saw those flowers in person, but they still managed to cheer me up!

He also became my hero by smuggling over the rest of that little cup of water that neither one of us knew if I was actually allowed to drink.

I don't think anything has ever felt or tasted so good as that cup of water! The cool liquid freed my tongue from the roof of my mouth and soothed my burning throat.

" How are you?"

"I think I'm OK. I haven't talked to anyone since the surgery, and I don't think anyone here speaks English."

Ahmed took my hand and kept me company in the darkness, both literal and figurative. We knew that I had survived, but not much more than that.

CHAPTER TWENTY-THREE

On My Death Bed?

At some point, movement outside my room caught my attention. There was a cute nurse bouncing along the hallway, grinning into my room. (I'm not exaggerating here... her reddish/gold curls were bouncing with her as she walked/skipped along.) Well, this was interesting. But then I noticed that she was not just smiling into my room. She was smiling in a particular direction...where Ahmed was sitting. Had he met her when he came into the hospital? Maybe asked her for directions? I let my questions bounce out of view with her, but before I knew it, she was there in my doorway with a machine in her hands and a HUGE smile for Ahmed. She put the machine on the windowsill and turned to look at him. I watched her eyes move over him, taking in his dark hair, his intense golden/green eyes, his perfect nose, his kissable lips, his sweet dimples, his chiseled jaw, his broad shoulders, his muscled arm, his strong hand... holding mine...

After a second to process what she was seeing, her eyes flew to mine, which I'm not afraid to admit, were probably not inviting. She whirled, curls flying, grabbed her machine, and literally ran out of the room. I never saw her or her machine again.

I turned my eyes, and attitude, on Ahmed, and would you believe he had a massive smile on his face. He thought it was FUNNY! Truth be told, he liked getting his fair share (or more) of admiration. He knew that people considered him handsome, and he kind of reveled in it. (Not to the extent of being arrogant about it, but there was no false humility here.) He was also proud of his "American girlfriend" and was happy to show me off whenever he had the chance. In this case, he got to do both, and he was loving it. I, on the other hand, was not.

But I wasn't too bothered, either. He had let me know long ago what he thought of girls who were focused solely on their appearance. Once, while looking at pictures from his job, I commented on a pretty girl. He made fun, saying that she walked around like, "Look at me. I'm so pretty." Apparently, she used her looks to get what she wanted, and he wasn't impressed.

In any case, Ahmed more than made up the incident as he left for the night. He kissed me good-bye and then asked,

"Do you want me to call your family?"

I was stunned! I never would have dreamed of asking him to call them for me. His English was wonderful, as was his Turkish, Arabic, and of course, Kurdish, but that's a lot of pressure! He would have to talk to my mom, and possibly my dad, and tell them about my surgery. I teared up as I asked him if he'd really do that for me. He smiled THAT smile at me, and that was the moment that I knew I loved him. My mom, who had thought that she would have to wait hours for word, probably had some pretty warm feelings for him at that moment, too!

CHAPTER TWENTY-FOUR

Vulnerability

At 3 o'clock in the morning, another set of torturers came to find me in the ICU. Thus began the worst night of my life so far. (As if the day had been a picnic!) This was definitely the most humiliating experience of my life, and I've toyed with not including it in this story because even now, the vulnerability of the moment brings tears to my eyes. But some of the most valuable lessons in life can be found in the most difficult experiences. We learn who we are and what we're capable of. That night, I came face to face with my own pride, need for control, and self-image.

They came to transport me to the x-ray room so that the doctors would be able to see if the operation was a success. I had been fading in and out of sleep for the last few hours, and I still couldn't move much more than my eyes. There were two of them, a sturdy but awkward-looking young guy and a tiny young nurse who looked like she was in fear for her life, and neither one spoke a word of English.

My surgeon had told me that someone would be coming, but I wouldn't say that I was expecting them. I wasn't thinking straight at 3 am. I was awoken by the wheels of the gurney as they pulled it up next to my bed and, without a word, began removing my blankets. (Ok, there may have been some words, but they were in Turkish, so they were wasted on me.) I desperately tried to cover myself with the flimsy hospital gown, not really sure what was happening. They literally dragged me off the side of the bed and onto the gurney using the sheet under me. As I was wheeled through the halls, the young guy kept staring openly at me with wide eyes and whispering, "*çok guzel.*" ('Very pretty' in Turkish.) I didn't want his, or any, eyes on me in this situation, but all I could do was lie there and wish that I was anywhere else.

When we got to the x-ray room, they wheeled me over next to what looked like a metal conveyor belt. (Think baggage reclaim area at an airport.) They would need to lift me up off of the gurney and then put me down onto the machine, which was only inches above the floor. I was mostly numb, so I didn't feel much pain, but I was terrified. I looked over at this tiny girl and wondered what would happen if she dropped me. From the expression on her face, she was having the same thoughts.

In that moment, I was exposed and completely powerless, feeling like a beached whale as they hoisted me off the gurney and swung/slid me onto the cold, hard metal platform. I kept my gaze down, refusing to look at those witnessing my shame. Just when I thought the pain and humiliation were almost over, without warning, they pulled the sheet out from under me. They unceremoniously flopped me onto my stomach, my hospital gown flying as they x-rayed from a different angle.

Up until now, I had been trying to be brave and dignified, but at this point, I lost it, and the tears started to fall. All the while, "çok guzel" was ringing in my mind. I wanted desperately to cover myself and hide, or crawl away and die, but all I could do was lie there at their mercy and pray that it would be over soon.

CHAPTER TWENTY-FIVE

Real Shame

Much more to my shame than any exposure I experienced while at the hospital that morning, I really hated that "çok guzel" guy. I felt that his words and gaze were inappropriate and made a really difficult situation nearly unbearable. I angrily wondered why he was working at the hospital in close contact with patients.

Back in my ICU bed in one piece, my righteous anger faded away and was replaced by shame. Once I could see past my own discomfort, I realized that I had made him the villain in my own mind just to be able to blame someone for my distress. The truth is that he didn't deserve any of my judgments.

I mentioned earlier that he seemed a bit awkward… In fact, I would be willing to bet that he has an intellectual disability. There was an air of innocence about him that I had refused to see. A good friend of mine, who spoke Turkish, later explained to me that "çok guzel" can also be a form of encouragement like "very nice, good job." And, if all of this wasn't enough, to be honest, his reaction to me wasn't exactly unheard of there in Turkey. They don't see many people with blond hair, blue-green eyes, and a splash of freckles, so I got some strong reactions while I was there.

Once I let my ego go, I was glad that the hospital employed people from various backgrounds. Later still, that "çok guzel" guy quite literally saved my life (or at least my back), and I found myself thanking God that he was there!

CHAPTER TWENTY-SIX

Good News

T he next morning, I woke up to my neurosurgeon, assistant neurosurgeon, and nurse's smiling faces. I doubt that I had ever been more relieved.

"Everything went well! How are you feeling?"

Kinder words have never been spoken. (At least not to me!) After hours going in and out of consciousness and wondering if all was well with all of the numbness below my shoulders, I was finally getting some information on my situation.

"We'll know more after we get the x-rays, but everything went great! Once we got in there, we could see how unstable your spine really was! Dr. Arslan will come back in a few hours to get you up out of bed."

I was so relieved, I thanked them by almost giving Dr. Arslan a heart attack…

CHAPTER TWENTY-SEVEN

On My Feet Again

I didn't do it on purpose! Once they had a chance to view the x-rays, my assistant surgeon came back to examine me and get me on my feet. What he didn't realize is that I'm a big wimp.

The first step was to put my brace on. He and my nurse turned me on my side, placed the brace under me, laid me back down on it, and connected and tightened the stays. Once I was safely strapped in, it was time to get up and test their work.

He put the handles on the side of the bed down… and I was fine.

He helped me turn onto my side… and I was fine.

He helped pull my legs up in a loose fetal position… and I was fine.

He even helped me get up into a seated position, and I was still mostly fine.

But then he asked me to do the impossible…and walk.

I clung to his hands as if to a life preserver while I shifted my legs and eased out onto the edge of the bed one inch at a time.

"OK, I need you to stand up."

It sounds like an easy enough thing to do… when you trust your body to support you. The truth is that I was terrified. I gingerly leaned forward and pushed my weight onto the balls of my feet. I got up with a lot of help from him and others. The pain that roared down my back when I simply shifted my weight to take a step forward stopped me in my tracks. I leaned back and crumpled onto the bed with a loud, "I can't."

From his expression, my doctor was horror-stricken, sure that something had gone terribly wrong with the surgery. I struggled to tell him what was wrong. Yes, there was pain, but it wasn't unbearable. But the fear? That was paralyzing. It was like walking out on a cliff, not knowing if my body would catch me when I fell. I felt broken, and I didn't know if I would ever feel whole again.

CHAPTER TWENTY-EIGHT

Unlikely Hero

Not long after putting my assistant neurosurgeon in a panic, I finally managed the first steps with my new and improved, fused back. It hurt... a lot. But I was able to manage a weak shuffle. This meant that I could leave the ICU torture chamber behind, and head back to my comfortable private room with a view.

Unfortunately, this also meant that I was once again reliant on the nurses for everything. They wanted me off the catheter as soon as possible to get me moving and make sure that my body was working properly. Unfortunately, that meant that I would have to call to get an escort to the toilet.

The nurse who answered my first call to get up and make the trip came in and raised the back of the bed for me. She took hold of my hands and was about to pull, straight up, when my "çok guzel" guy rushed into the room in a flurry of Turkish. My interpretation is that he was instructing her on how to help me. He showed her how to turn me onto my side first before helping me slowly swing my legs down the side of the bed. I probably felt as chagrined as she did. I should definitely have known better, even if she didn't. How long had I been dealing with back issues?

He had her support me on one side while he helped me up and bore my weight on the other. Between them, they walked me to the bathroom and then accompanied me back when I was ready.

I smiled at him as they got me settled. I was never able to have a conversation with him, thus the lack of a name, but I knew that he had saved me and my back that day. (I cringe to think what would have happened if he hadn't intervened! The direct pressure on my back from pulling straight up could have broken the stitches and perhaps damaged the work they had done in surgery.) I did my best to put all of the gratitude I felt into that smile. I hope he understood.

CHAPTER TWENTY-NINE

Trust

T
alking to my mom on the phone wasn't the only tricky situation I was about to put Ahmed through. My friend Jonathan had come to visit me at the hospital and had taken the key to my apartment to pick some things up for me. Unfortunately, he wasn't sure when he would able to get back to me. On the other hand, Ahmed had been visiting me every other day since I was checked into the hospital. He offered to get my things, but first, he needed to go to the restaurant where Jonathan was having dinner with some of our English teacher friends to get my key. I wasn't sure how Jonathan would treat Ahmed after his tone over the phone.

"How well do you really know this guy? Are you sure you can trust him?"

He may have thought that I was foolish for trusting Ahmed, but the fact was that I did. Ahmed had been there for me when no one else was. So I sent Ahmed into the lion's den, so to speak, and once again, he took it in stride. He met them in a neighborhood restaurant, introduced himself, and retrieved my key. I was impressed. I get nervous entering crowded places even when I'm meeting my own friends, let alone trying to find someone else's. I'm sure the foreigners stood out, but still.

*****

If you ever want to know how well someone speaks a language, just try giving them instructions over the phone. I was trying to explain what I needed from home and where to find it. Who knew he didn't know the word 'wardrobe'? I tried desperately to remember where I had left things, and then tried to guide him to them one step at a time. He slowly, very slowly, gathered the items I hoped would make my stay in the hospital a little more comfortable. He didn't balk at the teddy bear, but the pajamas gave him pause.

"But…. you'll be… almost naked." (His voice broke adorably on "naked.")

"Honey, they help me get up and take me to the bathroom, clean my back, and give me a shower. They've already seen everything there is to see."

There was a pause, and then,

"Yeah, OK."

The funny thing is that they were long pants and a tank top. I guess it was the spaghetti straps, or maybe just the idea that someone else would see me in my jammies.

CHAPTER THIRTY

Cinderella

O nce I got my feet under me, I settled into hospital life
for the next week. I figured out that the change of the
guard each morning was because it was a teaching
hospital. When the shift changed, the old and the new nurses,
along with everyone shadowing the nurses, would visit each
patient and get a rundown of the situation. (The run down was
in Turkish, which I understood very little of. I did understand
the panic in their eyes when told that I was a foreigner who
only spoke English.) The first time they came in, I wilted under
their curious gazes. I was keenly aware that I was reliant on
them for everything. There was nothing that I could do for
myself.

Even though I didn't have much control physically, I realized
that I could still control how I treated others. I could easily
have just given in to my misery and made everyone around me
miserable too, or I could be the kind of person I wanted to be,
even here. I found a smile at 4 am for the nurse who came to
take my vitals. I chose to laugh instead of cry when my teddy
bear fell while a nurse was fixing my IV and I sprayed blood
across the floor trying to catch it. (I looked at her first to gauge

her reaction before we both broke out into giggles.) And while I may not know much Turkish, 'thank you,' was one of the first things I had learned, and it made the nurses giggle to hear me say it.

In the days that followed, a few brave souls came to the front to try out the few words of English they knew on me. Everyone was thoroughly impressed when I was able to make sense of what they said and respond. Meanwhile, the shy smiled and waved at me from behind the others.

The most fun we had was when a couple of nurses helped me put on the back brace/corset/straight jacket I would be taking home with me. (I had one already, but this one was extra supportive.) There were strings at the back that needed to be tightened, rigid supports that needed to be arranged to keep the back straight, hooks in the front that needed to be fastened, and straps going up either side that needed to be synched down. With all of the to-do, we ended up giggling up a storm as the two of them practically joined me in my hospital bed while pushing, pulling, and getting me all suited up. It was a bit like I imagine Cinderella must have felt while being dressed by the mice, only a bit more… confining. (And my mice were bigger!) In the end, I was safe and secure, and we were wiping tears of laughter from our eyes.

CHAPTER THIRTY-ONE

Turkish Bathing

Eventually, the day came when I needed to prepare myself for my first shower after the surgery. I had mixed feelings; the thought of being clean was extremely welcome, but the idea of sharing that moment with someone else was not. Actually, I was a little frustrated. I was feeling stronger. Why wouldn't they let me take a shower on my own? What I didn't realize was that much of the strength that I thought I felt actually came from the brace supporting my back. Stripped of that support, I was soon timidly sitting and allowing myself to be washed while my muscles trembled with exhaustion. Sitting there with tubes hanging from my shaking limbs, I understood what it meant to fully rely on someone else. I was putty in her hands.

This would have been a nightmare for the girl who used to cry with embarrassment at getting a bra fitting, but fortunately, I was no longer that girl.

Months before, a friend's visit to Istanbul had taken me to one of the iconic Turkish experiences: the Turkish bath. The one we visited was one of the oldest in the city, boasting ancient stonework surrounding a large pool of water. There were ledges all around to sit on, and more private bathing stations with intricate sinks where you could gather bowls of warm water to pour over yourself while lounging in the steam. You could wear a bathing suit, but most people went around topless without a care. There were different services available, from just relaxing on your own to being washed and exfoliated by one of the attendants. I had decided that if I was going to have the Turkish bath experience, I would accompany my friend and try to enjoy it to the fullest.

It was actually fun. The other ladies there were receiving the same pampering, so there was no need to be shy. The assistants were professionals, and while they were friendly, they were also matter-of-fact. They had a job to do. I was able to relax amid thoughts of the history and culture of this place, and when I left there, I felt cleaner and more relaxed than I had ever been.

After being lathered, scraped and buffed by a complete stranger in front of at least 10 other ladies in the same predicament, being washed by a nurse seemed almost natural.

*****

The next day, my personal nurse came and took me to the cafe for coffee as a reward for good behavior and showering. Well…I could tell from her raised eyebrow that she would have preferred me to have tea, but they had Lavazza coffee, so my choice was made.

We relaxed on the covered patio outside and enjoyed the sunlight, fresh air, and easy conversation. I was finally starting to feel like myself again. My nurse was so thrilled at my progress that she asked if we could stop by my neurosurgeon's office to show me off.

Their praise made me blush, even though it was more their doing than anything I had done. Life was starting to seem brighter.

CHAPTER THIRTY-TWO

Going Home

My stay in the hospital came to an abrupt halt.
I woke up from a nap and looked down to find my hand swollen like an ugly purple balloon. I desperately rang for the nurses, and they came to take the needle out. The head nurse was able to explain to me in English what had happened between admonishing looks for the nurses on duty. The needle had slipped from the vein, and the saline had built up in the tissue. I don't know if it was a reaction to the saline, or if I just hadn't really looked at my hands in days, but it seemed that my hands and wrists were covered in vivid bruises in places I didn't remember having been poked. (Many of them were probably from the surgery.) When the nurses came back in to stick me with yet another needle, I crossed my arms in panic and asked for my doctors. I couldn't hold back my tears; I had had enough.

After having some time to get my composure back, one of those hunky nurses I mentioned earlier turned his charming smile on me and talked me into allowing them to reinsert the IV. But before they could, my neurosurgeon rushed in. We talked for a while about what the bruises came from and how I was feeling. (I had been off my meds for a little while at this point.)

"I wasn't going to send you home yet, but since you're doing OK without the IV, maybe it's time."

And so they started the preparations to send me home.

The last thing I remember is a nurse who, up until that point, had not uttered a word to me, coming nervously to my bedside and saying in very halting English, "Beautiful smile."

The next morning when I left, they didn't want me to go, and I must say I felt a little sad leaving them behind. What I couldn't know was that the hardest part of my recovery was still to come.

CHAPTER THIRTY-THREE

Post-Op Depression

Being in the hospital was dreary, but coming home was truly bleak. In the hospital, I had frequent visitors and calls from home to keep my spirits up. Ahmed was there every other day, and my team of doctors and my nurse came to see me several times a day and exclaimed over how well I was doing.

The first week back home, I was confined to my apartment to rest and recover. It felt like a prison, and all I wanted to do was go outside. But by the time I was finally supposed to go out for short walks, my desire to do that, or anything else, had faded away. Regular everyday tasks, like getting out of bed, getting dressed, eating, and interacting with people became monumental tasks that I couldn't face.

Depression isn't a stranger to my family, and I had dealt with it myself in the past. Still, I was totally unprepared for the wave of despair that engulfed me. My logical mind told me that I had so many things to be thankful for, but I felt anything but logical or grateful. I couldn't find the energy to care, about anything. In the past, my depression was like the sun going behind clouds; everything was just a little less vivid. But the sun always came out again. This, this was like being trapped in a dark pit, with no way to claw my way out.

But I was lucky. Ahmed kept me human by visiting when he could and giving me a reason to get out of bed, shower, wear something other than pajamas, tidy up the apartment a little, and smile. (I even managed to wear makeup a time or two!) I also had family and friends who reached out to me. Jonathan, in particular, came down to walk with me every couple of days even though he was busy with his own life. He got me out of my head and kept me connected to the real world, even though it wasn't always easy. He didn't get angry when I didn't answer one of his many calls, but instead told me that when I heard that ringing, it meant that someone cared about me. (He understood because he had been there himself.)

I was also lucky to have my neurosurgeon. Not only was he an amazing surgeon, but he took the time to listen to what I was going through and answer my many questions. When I told him of my lack of appetite and depression, he told me something that I had not been able to identify in my own thinking; I felt unsafe.

As soon as he said it, it made perfect sense! I had a seven-inch incision down my back on top of the previous operation's four-inch scar, and the muscles in my back had been cut not once, but twice. The truth is, when I didn't have the brace on, I felt like I was starring in an alien film, but in this one, the alien would claw its way out my lower back. It felt like the staples were the only thing holding me together, and when they were gone, I wondered what was fighting against the strain I could feel in my back. The worst part is that I didn't notice any improvement. I had only ever had minor injuries/illnesses where after treatment, each day I would feel a little better and a little stronger. But day after day, I felt the same, like I was going to fall apart at any moment.

One image comes to mind as I write about this feeling of being unsafe. I remember taking a trip into the city on the metro once I was able to get around again. I was all trussed up in my back brace, but as I stepped onto the top of the escalator, I felt like a weeble. (If you're not familiar with a weeble, its a children's toy with a rounded bottom that rocks back and forth before settling back upright.) I clung to the handrail, sure that I would pitch forward and crash down the escalator at any moment, taking innocent bystanders with me. I didn't fall that day, but I still get vertigo when climbing down stairs, and the handrails that I used to ignore have become my constant companions.

CHAPTER THIRTY-FOUR

See Me

I lived for Ahmed's visits, but at the same time, I didn't want him to see me like this. I was afraid that maybe if he saw me with all of my flaws, which now included a back that looked like it belonged to Frankenstein's monster, he would decide that that two-hour trip to see me wasn't really worth it after all. He deserved way more credit than that.

As soon as he got me settled in back home, he asked me what we needed to do to help me get well. With eyes downcast in embarrassment, I told him that I had to clean the wound, but that no matter how I twisted and turned, it was nearly impossible for me to clean and bandage it myself.

"I can do it!"

I REALLY did not want him to see the jagged, stapled cut that spanned my lower back. Without hesitation, he took the iodine from me and patted the bed invitingly. With a sigh, I laid down on my stomach and explained what he needed to do while he took the old bandage off. He gently tended to my wound, and once he had a clean bandage covering it, he leaned forward and kissed my injury, just like my mom used to do for my skinned knees. He was rewarded with a flood of tears that there were no words to explain, but he understood. From that evening forward, he took it as his responsibility to look after my hurts.

*****

This wasn't the last time that my insecurities plagued our relationship. One night, I wiggled away from his caress on my tummy, saying,

"Don't play with my fat!"

"I like it!"

"Why?"

...

"I don't know... I just do."

Truth be told, I loved his flaws, too. He was thoroughly intimidating with his good looks, his infuriating (at times) charm, and his keen intelligence. Without his skinny legs (his words), and the receding hairline that he attempted to cover with a strategic cut and comb, he wouldn't have seemed human. But despite his physical beauty and the reactions that he got because of it, he maintained a sweet humility that I probably didn't fully appreciate while we were together. Insecurities can interfere with that kind of thing.

One "flaw" that I adored was the way his eyes crinkled when

he smiled. He was very self-conscious about it, which was apparent in all the pictures I saw of him. He knew that his eyes were one of his best features, so he wanted to show them off. In photos, he always trained an intense gaze on the camera or had just enough of a smile to show his dimples without squinting his eyes. In any case, he avoided giving a real smile. At least he did until he realized how much I loved his big smile. I'll never forget his excitement when he returned from a fishing trip with his friends on the Bosphorus. As soon as he got into the apartment, he raced over to my computer and said he had something to show me. Soon, I saw his huge smile and crinkled, but still sparkling, green eyes set against a background of blue-green sea and his favorite green shirt. (There may have been a bucket of tiny fish in there somewhere as well.)

"Honey, you're really smiling! Look how handsome you are!"

"I know... I took it for you."

I don't know if I can really explain how touching this was. Not only was Ahmed thinking of me while he was out with his friends, but he did something that he didn't really like doing (smiling in a picture) because he knew I would like it.

I had always dreamed of meeting someone who would cherish me, but years alternating between the dating game and being single had destroyed some of those childhood dreams. Yet here he was, loving me completely, flaws and all. Not only that, but he was willing to confront his own "flaws" and try new things to make me happy. In him, I found the strength to believe that what I had been looking for was not only possible, but it was standing right in front of me, looking at me like I was everything he had ever hoped for and more.

CHAPTER THIRTY-FIVE

Love Without the I Love Yous

My affectionate nature, and the cultural expectations I grew up with, made it easy for me to tell Ahmed how I was feeling. He would respond to my "I love you"s with "I love you too," but he never said it first. Even so, nearly everything he did made me feel loved and respected.

When I opened the door, and he pulled me into a bear hug with an "I missed you!" I would just giggle and snuggle in. Between my doctor's orders to stay at home to heal and Ahmed 's desire to see me whenever he possibly could, it was never more than a few days that we didn't see each other. But from his greetings, you'd think we hadn't seen each other for months! It felt like I love you.

He also had a strange habit of play biting me on the cheek. Don't worry, he wasn't crazy, and it didn't hurt! He knew very well how odd it was… He'd say, "I don't know why I do that. I only do it to people that I…care about. I used to do it to my sister, too." Another of his favorite sayings was, "I've never been this comfortable with anyone!" Apparently, there are about a million ways of saying I love you, and many of them don't require words.

When his sister got married, he was excited to show me ALL of the pictures and ALL of the videos. He explained some of their wedding traditions, such as the gifts of gold jewelry given to the bride as a way to bring prosperity to the couple. He pointed out each member of his family and told me stories about each of them. He had even had a picture taken of him standing by the wedding altar, all sharp suit and sad eyes. I wondered if that one was taken especially for me too. But I've gotten ahead of the story!

When Ahmed told me of his family, he painted the picture of a loving, but conservative Muslim family. I had learned early on that Syrian Kurdish people tend to marry within their own clan. He was thrilled that my name Laureen has a Kurdish variation: Lorin. It gave him the opening to tell his family about his American friend, who had a Kurdish name. For him, I love yous were for the one you would marry, and his family would have had a hard time accepting me.

"If things were different… if my family was OK… I could be happy with you in America."

If only.

CHAPTER THIRTY-SIX

In Pictures

As the days passed, our relationship was documented through pictures. One of the reasons for this was that we both knew that Ahmed might not always be there. His answer to that was to collect memories to hold onto in the difficult times to come.

One of those memories was a nighttime outing to Levent Tower, one of the tallest buildings in Istanbul. From the glass-enclosed roof of the tower, we stared out at the lights of Istanbul, expanding out and receding into the distance. There were markers for each direction with a list of well-known places in that direction and how far away they were. There were also pictures and facts from many of those places displayed on the wall. Ahmed was excited to take a photo of each display, and I wished that we could travel to each location together.

We snuggled in for selfies, asked others to take our photo, and then Ahmed suggested getting a themed picture taken in the shop as well. As the cashier showed us the two pictures that we took against different backgrounds, I had a hard time deciding which one I liked the most. I asked him to choose and then walked away to look at the items in the gift shop.

As I was perusing the shelves, I accidentally knocked over a few postcards. I stood staring down at them, trying to decide how I could convince my back, and the accompanying brace, to bend down to retrieve them. I knew that I wouldn't be able to bend straight forward. Maybe I could kneel to the side and reach over to pick them up? Then the real trouble would begin. How was I going to get back up? My back sometimes got stuck in one position when it was bent awkwardly, and the muscles in my back were next to useless this soon after surgery. I eyed the closest shelf, mentally measuring the distance and taking in the thin metal. I didn't think I trusted it enough to help me pull myself up. I tried to keep the tears back, but it was hard to do in the face of my helplessness in such a simple situation. I was ashamed to ask for help (again).

After a few minutes, he walked over to me with two pictures in his hands and a big smile on his face.

"What do you think?"

I instantly wished that I had only shown an interest in one picture. I knew he didn't have much money, but that never kept him from trying to give me everything I wanted. He had printed both his favorite and mine. There we were on the page, smiling against some of the most famous backdrops of Istanbul. I tried to get him to take one, but he said that they were for me to remember. (Like I would ever forget!) As he reached down to retrieve my fallen postcards, I made a mental note to scan the pictures and send them to him so he could keep the memories close, too.

Our next stop was an Imax virtual ride that featured a helicopter flight over and through the most famous sites in

Istanbul. As our eyes traveled over the tops of domed mosques and the iconic Bosphorus bridge, Ahmed filmed the journey.

It was there that I learned of his love of videos. In fact, I was soon to learn that he was a bit of an amateur video journalist. When we returned home, he showed me some videos he had taken. One, in particular, gave me more insight into why he had come to Turkey. A couple of days before he traveled to Istanbul, there was a protest in one of the main squares of his hometown. He had taken a video, intent on sharing it with the world. From what I could see, it was a large group of mostly young men, but their words were lost on me. They weren't doing anything threatening or aggressive, just peacefully protesting. Suddenly, shots rang out in the video, and everyone, including my cameraman, ducked and ran for cover.

In my American naiveté, I asked, "Were those rubber bullets?" They were not. "Who was shooting?" The police. "Were they shooting in the air?" No. "But what if someone died?" He just shrugged.

The tears came before I even understood exactly what I was seeing in the footage. I sat, staring in shock and struggled to come to grips with the fact that I could have lost him right there, without ever knowing him.

Never have I been in a position where I feared law enforcement. My dad was a guard at a prison in my hometown for over twenty years. I've always seen them as protectors: the good guys. Yet Ahmed had grown up in a place where law enforcement couldn't always be trusted, and here they were shooting live ammunition into a group of unarmed young men to stop them from coming together to protest the war and the government's seizure of parts of their city.

CHAPTER THIRTY-SIX

"I shouldn't have shown you that."

He was angry with himself for upsetting me, and I was angry that a government could treat its people this way.

A couple of days after that video was shot, Ahmed had made his way to Istanbul.

CHAPTER THIRTY-SEVEN

Giving Thanks

Teaching in a private university and living on the European side of the city, it was easy to forget that I was living in a Muslim country. That is, until I headed out to buy alcohol. (Which I didn't do often, I swear!) Some occasions do lend themselves to a toast or two, and our expat Thanksgiving get together was definitely one of those. While I waited for Ahmed to make his way over to my side of town, I went down to buy a bottle of wine to take with us. The price strained my already diminished bank account, but I consoled myself with the fact that it was a special occasion.

When Ahmed arrived, I showed him what I had bought. His expression saddened.

"I don't like wine. I want to toast, too."

With that, we headed back down to the liquor store with the offending bottle of wine. He explained our situation to the shop keeper (his Turkish is MUCH better than mine, meaning he actually speaks it), and we arranged to return the wine and put the money toward something else that we both liked. He chose a bottle of vodka and a couple of cans of Red Bull. We were both shocked at the total at the register, even after taking off the money I had already paid. With a troubled expression, Ahmed bravely handed the clerk his bank card, and my heart constricted because I knew he couldn't afford it. (But neither could I, not that he would have let me pay.) When we got to our friends' apartment, their eyebrows raised at the sight of the vodka. When I thought about it later, I had a feeling the only time Ahmed had ever had alcohol was when he was working for the tour agency. He had once told me of a guest who had bought him a drink at one of the night clubs in Istanbul. The importance of this, his first toast, became clear to me.

*****

At the Thanksgiving celebration, I walked around, introducing Ahmed to all of my friends. His eyes jumped from face to face nervously, but he only spoke to answer their questions politely. Once he had settled in a bit, I left him to socialize while I helped my friends in the kitchen.

Soon after, we put out the call for everyone to fill their plates. Once I was finished dishing out green beans to everyone, I filled my own plate and headed into the living room where everyone was gathered. I was a bit disappointed when I scanned the room for Ahmed and found him sitting between two others on the couch. Why hadn't he saved me a seat? I moved to another couch where there was still space, and his eyes widened with surprise. As I sat down, he rushed over and sat down at my feet.

Now I was uncomfortable for a very different reason. If my back had been able to handle it, I would have gotten down there with him. But I knew it couldn't.

"Honey, you can sit over there, it's OK. I just can't sit on the floor with my back."

"That's OK. I want to be here with you. I always sit on the floor at home."

I was still uncomfortable, hoping that my nearby feet weren't ruining his first Thanksgiving meal. But I soon forgot my discomfort in the company of people that I cared about and warmed by familiar foods that I hadn't tasted for months. It wasn't the family Thanksgiving that I was used to, and I missed them terribly, but it was a special Istanbul Thanksgiving.

CHAPTER THIRTY-EIGHT

Christmas Boots

U nable to support themselves in Istanbul, Ahmed's family had returned to Syria to come up with another plan to build a new future. A couple of weeks before Christmas, Ahmed left to visit them with promises to return for the holiday. Meanwhile, I spent my time preparing the apartment for our first Christmas together.

While Turkey is a Muslim country, Christmas does show up in certain corners of Istanbul under the guise of 'Noel.' Bakeries fill their window displays with red and green lights and smiling Santa faces. Neighborhood office supply shops offer small artificial trees, strings of miniature lights, and other decorations. By this time, my monthly salary didn't leave much to work with after converting most of it into American dollars to pay bills back home. I set about trying to find affordable gifts and decorations to make the holiday a memorable one.

Part of my salary included a small stipend for lunches at work. It was uploaded onto a card that was accepted at the university cafeteria and a few outside restaurants, including Starbucks. I went there in search of gifts, thinking that Ahmed could take it in his luggage if he left Istanbul. I approached the cashier with a reindeer mug for Ahmed and a white mug with a candy cane handle for myself. "You can't use your card for these." Embarrassed, I paid with the last of the money in my bank account and headed home to decorate the mugs and stash them under our little Christmas tree.

I was working on the finishing touch for our tree, a handmade star, when I heard his knock. I opened the door to find him standing there, boots caked with mud, shoulders bowed with exhaustion, but eyes sparkling with joy. He stepped in and pulled me close.

"I missed you," Ahmed sighed into my neck.

"I missed you too! Come and sit down. Are you tired?"

He sat and began prying off his boots.

"Yes. It's been a long night and day. Look at my boots!"

"What happened?"

"I had to sneak across the border to get here. Even though I have my passport, the border checkpoint is dangerous for us. Two men were killed there last month."

"Are you OK? Did you cross alone?"

"I'm OK, just tired. I was supposed to cross with my brother, but he's leaving tomorrow, and I wanted to be with you for Christmas. I went with a guide, but we had to turn back three times. Finally, at around midnight, we climbed the fence. We walked for hours without lights until we reached Mersin. That's where I called you."

I was torn between concern for him and the lump that had formed in my throat at hearing what he had gone through to get back. Christmas wasn't his holiday, but it was important to me, which made it important to him.

CHAPTER THIRTY-NINE

Christmas Star

H e put his boots and luggage off to the side, and then joined me on the couch. I showed him a star that I was trying, and failing, to glue together for our little Christmas tree.

"Honey, I'm so tired now, but if you can wait while I take a nap, we can do it together."

With a smile and a kiss, I sent him off for his nap. He had silenced me yet again with surprise and left me floating in a sense of wonder that he would want to help me with my 'artsy stuff.'

If you're not an artistic person, it may be difficult to understand how deeply his simple statement touched me. This was the first time a boyfriend had taken an interest in my creative side. (And it's an important side! My undergraduate degree was in Fine Art, and that's what had led me to study Italian language and study abroad in Italy. That trip was a dream come true, and it started the love affair with travel that had eventually brought me to Turkey...twice.)

Many years earlier, I had tried to share this side of myself with a longtime boyfriend by showing him some of my drawings. I was quickly dismissed with, "That's nice, Laureen." It may seem trivial, but it broke my heart. It sounded like something you would tell a child to get her to go away. I had bared part of my soul, only to find indifference, bordering on annoyance, on the other side. At that point, I felt that my ex just wanted a warm body next to him, not necessarily me. And I started looking for the door. I also became guarded about what I shared and who I shared it with.

But this, this was something new. And even though I giggled to myself at the thought of Ahmed's thick, clumsy fingers trying to hold the sides of the star together long enough for the glue to take hold, I was touched by his desire to be a part of even that side of my life.

While Ahmed slept upstairs, I kept trying to finish our Christmas star. My eyes kept straying to Ahmed's mud-encrusted boots. I wondered if I was worth the risks that he had taken, and imagined what could have happened. If he had been hurt or killed, would I have ever known? He was here now, and I was humbled by the sacrifices he had made to get here and the way he valued every part of me.

CHAPTER FORTY

Building New Traditions

Once Ahmed woke up, we laid a blanket down on the floor near the tree and sat down to open gifts and celebrate Christmas Eve. The tile beneath us was a little cold and hard even with the blanket, but it made Ahmed happy to sit this way. I have to admit that it allowed us to sit close while still facing each other, making it a very intimate experience. With the lights from the tree, a fake fire on the computer, and Christmas carols from my childhood playing in the background, we told stories as we peeked into boxes and bags. Ahmed grinned as he told me the story of the sweets he had brought.

"When I was a boy, my grandfather used to bring these treats every time he came to visit from Turkey. He would bring a whole one just for me!"

He laughed, holding up what looked like a home-made fruit wrap. I loved its sweet, fruity texture. I was less enthusiastic about the other sweet. I think it could be described as candied nuts, but not candied the way I would have expected. It was a rope of walnuts encased in a candied sleeve. To be honest, they tasted pretty good, especially for walnuts. The problem is that when I looked at them, all I could think of was sausage links. I hate sausage links. Luckily, the fruit roll was plenty, so we shared that, and I left most of the walnuts for him. (And he didn't complain!)

He smiled at his mug, rushing to wash both of them and make tea for us. It had become our morning tradition: black tea and Nutella on Turkish cookies for breakfast. He liked to spread the chocolate on the cookies for me and sometimes feed them to me as well. It always ended in giggling, with Nutella all over our hands and faces like kids.

He told me about his visit home while we ate. They had had to close their pharmacy long before because everything was too expensive to supply. Part of his hometown had been taken over by the military, and they were only allowed electricity for about an hour each day. He and his family slept in the same room for warmth, and they struggled to get the food they needed to feed their family. Even so, they were happy to be there together. As I mentioned previously, Ahmed's younger sister had married a Kurdish man who was already established in Europe. A new dream of bringing the family together in Europe was taking shape. It would be Ahmed's job to make it happen.

CHAPTER FORTY-ONE

Celebration

A t the end of the year, the university that I worked for had a dinner party to thank its employees for their work throughout the year. (It felt like a Christmas/New Year's party, but they wouldn't actually say that... We were in Turkey, after all.)

Ahmed had had to work on New Year's Eve. I celebrated with friends and we had to settle for a phone call to welcome the new year. I thought this dinner party might make up for that a bit, but our evening got off to a rough start.

I was standing outside the bus (in silent protest), nervously waiting for Ahmed under the angry gaze of our van driver.

"Can we wait just a few more minutes? He's on his way."

I was just getting ready to send him a text saying that we had to leave without him when he came around the corner and rushed toward us.

"You're all dressed up! Why didn't you tell me to dress up?"

...

"I thought I did..."

As we settled into our seats, I realized that I hadn't actually told him that he should dress up. I told him it was a dinner party and assumed that he would know what that meant. It must have been a bit of a shock for him! I had curled my hair and was wearing contacts, makeup, and fancy clothes. This rarely happened!

"You look very handsome, don't worry!" I told him with a smile.

He actually had dressed up (in my opinion). Yes, he was wearing blue jeans, but he also had a nice white shirt and a gray blazer. I think he would have worn a full suit or even a tuxedo if I had told him where we were going!

*****

The dinner party was held in a space that felt like a museum. There was vintage machinery displayed throughout the building amidst dark wood furnishings and twinkling lights. It felt like a magical place and a magical night. We gathered together for drinks, laughter, and pictures. Ahmed was much more at home with my friends this time because he remembered them from Thanksgiving.

There was a brief hiccup as I was forced to choose between the Turkish teacher table and the *yabancı* (foreigner) table. It wasn't a choice I liked to make because it was a choice between friends. I said my hellos to everyone, and then we sat down at a huge round table with the other expats to share a meal. It felt so good to be here with friends again after so much time alone recovering. Now we were here together, celebrating the highs and lows, and Ahmed was a part of it. My world felt right.

After dinner, a band got ready, and an area was cleared for dancing. Once a few couples had gone out on the dance floor, Ahmed reached out his hand and asked me to dance. As he took me into his arms, he whispered,

"I've never done this before."

"You've never danced?"

"Not like this… not with a girl."

Apparently, his experience with dancing was limited to holding hands with other men and boys while dancing in a circle. Luckily, he was a natural, and he loved every minute of it! (In fact, I couldn't get him off the dance floor!) He was smiling from ear to ear, his adorable dimples flashing for all to see.

They played Turkish and American music, so it wasn't long before they played something more his style. I danced around the circle with him and my friends for a song or two and then bowed out to sit and watch (and rest). As I watched them all dance together, these people that I loved, my heart was filled with pride and happiness. There were no divisions of class, ethnicity, gender, or sexual orientation on that dance floor; there was simply a moment of joy shared.

Soon I was pulled back into the group, and there was nowhere else I wanted to be.

CHAPTER FORTY-TWO

Going Home?

It was still dark outside as our taxi made its way through the slush and rain. In trying to be among the first in line, we had arrived before the US consulate actually opened. There was no sign of a line, so we slogged across the street to have tea while we waited for the office to open.

The tea and the atmosphere were warm and relaxing, especially in contrast to the oppressive weather outside. But we had official business to take care of, so we soon headed back to face rejection.

I felt a little bit like I imagine parents feel on the first day of school. As we walked back, I ran a critical eye over him, taking in his hair and the button-down shirt he had worn for the occasion. His eyes darted around, giving away his nervousness.

"Just be yourself! They'll love you as much as I do! I'll be right here with you!"

Which I was… until we ran into an unmoveable security guard.

"No one can go with him past this point."

"But I'm the one sponsoring him."

"I'm sorry."

He didn't look sorry.

I was crushed. How could I help him if I wasn't there? I thought they would at least want to hear about my family and me and our plans for the visit, but they didn't want to know me at all.

I took a deep breath, knowing this was a battle I couldn't win.

"OK, I'll wait in the cafe. Good luck!"

I slogged back across the street to order a second cup of tea and obsess.

*****

By this time, I had returned to teaching at the university, and it was almost time for our winter break. I had asked my mom if I could bring Ahmed home with me. She was happy to have him, and even wrote a letter in support of his visa request, but it would be the US government that would ultimately decide if I could take him home to meet my family.

Before his appointment, we had sat for hours, completing all of the paperwork and daydreaming about what we would do while we were in the US. I wanted to show him San Francisco, and he was excited to experience Las Vegas. Plus, there were destinations closer to home: beautiful Lake Tahoe and the small town where I grew up.

He had no intention of staying in the US. Most of his family didn't speak English, and they wanted their whole family to be together. (His sister had already married and moved to Europe, and was living within a Kurdish community there.) Ahmed had convinced his family that getting a visa to go to the US would help him get other visas later. (Surely if the Americans trusted him, everyone else would too, right?)

*****

I had barely had time to order my second cup of tea when he walked in with his shoulders and eyes down. All of the time and money that we had put into that application, and they literally glanced at him and his nationality and dismissed him within seconds. They didn't even talk to him! I was ashamed. They couldn't even extend him an ounce of courtesy, a moment of their time to treat him like a human being! I was the first American that he had ever really known, and now this dismissive jerk was the second. I kept telling him that not all Americans are like that, but I think I was trying to remind myself, not convince him. He wasn't mad, and he wasn't at all surprised. Just like with so many other things, he calmly accepted it as the way it was.

CHAPTER FORTY-THREE

Déjà Vu

"Do you want to go to the Syrian restaurant for lunch?"

Did I? We had only been talking about it for months! We jumped on the minibus, the subway, one tram, and then another to get back to his side of town and the restaurant he had been telling me about since we first met. It wasn't the fanciest restaurant ever, but the huge smiles on the workers' faces made me feel welcome (if a little shy).

Once we sat down, Ahmed and I put our heads together over a menu while he tried to explain the different dishes.

"What's your favorite? That's what I want to try."

Ahmed ordered for us... and ordered... and ordered. I was shocked as they brought dish after dish to the table. How were we ever going to eat all this food? As each plate arrived, he told me the name of the dish and the ingredients. The food was delicious, and we chatted while we ate. I was enjoying our afternoon together, but he didn't seem as lively as he usually was. His smile wasn't as frequent as I was used to, and he kept dropping his gaze.

On our way out, he bought me a bag of spices that he had taught me to add to olive oil to put on bread for breakfast.

"Do you mind if we go to a music store? I need to get something for my cousin."

"Sure."

The store was beautiful, filled with inlaid Turkish guitars and drums. He paid for the guitar strings, and then stopped me to take my picture amidst the lovely instruments. Outside the shop, we stopped for a selfie, and again I wondered if something was going on. Why was he so camera happy today?

"Let's go get coffee."

I followed as he led the way further into town. We climbed a hill and turned back to look down on the Bosphorus and the lights of old Istanbul. We stood there in each other's arms for a while, enjoying each other's company and the beauty of this amazing place. Then we were on our way again, and soon he had brought me to the Lavazza shop at the base of Galata Tower, where we had had our first date. I was delighted to be there with him again, but now, the warning bells were really going off.

After coffee, we headed up Istiklal Street, moving toward the subway. We stopped to buy some *hammam* (Turkish bath) towels for my family visit that was coming up in January. I found a Turkish towel and soap set for my niece, and he bought one for his friend's wife. At one point, he asked me to wait a few minutes for him. I did a little window shopping while he ran his errand, still highly suspicious and a little concerned. He returned a little while later, with a dejected look on his face.

"I wanted to buy something special for you, but I couldn't find one that I thought you would like."

"You don't need to buy me anything!"

"But I want to. Come with me."

He led me into a sporting goods store where he promptly chose a pair of Real Madrid shorts.

"Do you like these?"

*****

Just so you know, Real Madrid isn't my team. But there's a little back story here. My favorite soccer team is the Italian team Juventus. I had been lucky enough to go to one of their games while living in Turin. It was my first time experiencing the European love of soccer. I've loved Juventus from then on, even through scandal and demotion. I've followed their progress more than I have any other sports team. On a more recent visit to Turin, I had bought a pair of men's Juventus shorts and kept them with me wherever I went. That meant that they were with me in Istanbul, and Ahmed often wore them when he was at my place. I think it was a little bit of a struggle for him to wear them the first couple of times because he felt like a traitor to his team, but he seemed to become strangely attached to them. I think he was hoping that I would become similarly attached to these new shorts that represented his own team, and him in turn.

*****

My thoughts were jumbled as we made our way back home. Once there, we settled onto the couch, and I turned to ask him,

"Are you leaving?"

…

"Yes."

"When?"

Silence…

"Are you leaving tomorrow?"

"Yes."

"…Why didn't you tell me?" (I have to admit, my voice broke on that last part.)

"I tried to tell you… but I couldn't."

Shocked and needing to escape the situation, I made my way up to the loft and started gathering his things to pack them.

"Don't!"

"I'm just trying to help you pack."

"Do you want me to leave now?" (Now it was his voice that cracked.)

"No."

He took my hand and led me back to the couch, where he told me the whole story. His parents had asked him to travel to Costa Rica, and then on to Europe. Apparently, some members of the Kurdish community in Syria shared how they were able to relocate. As I mentioned, Ahmed's parents wanted desperately to move to Europe to be with their friends and family. The problem was getting there. Their savings were slowly melting away, and it was becoming more and more impossible to live in their hometown. They had heard that someone they knew had made it to Europe through Costa Rica. Now it was his turn to try. Once there, he would need to gain refugee status, find a job and a home for the family, and then start the paperwork to bring the rest over. No pressure there!

With the pain that we were both feeling, it was impossible not to argue. Up until now, our only disagreements had been about me not telling him to dress up and about how to cook eggs. This argument hurt.

"That's why I haven't been saying I love you. I didn't want you to get attached."

"So now you don't love me? It was all just a lie?"

"Please don't say that."

There was something that I hadn't told him yet, something that had been weighing on my mind for a few weeks, but that I hadn't been able to say to him. I didn't think it was likely, but,

"There's a chance that I might be pregnant."

He looked broken. "But a child needs to be with his father."

"And otherwise, he's better off dead? I wouldn't do that. Not for you, not for anyone."

He hadn't said anything about abortion, but that's where my mind went when he talked about not being able to be there for a child. I needed him to know that it wasn't an option for me.

"Please don't let this be the biggest mistake of my life."

I looked at him and shrugged, feeling helpless. It was beyond my control.

"I don't really think I am pregnant, but there's a small chance. I haven't had my period this month."

He reached out and pulled me into a bear hug.

*****

Later that night, wrapped in each other's arms, we shared more honesty than we had all evening.

"If you don't love me, you have a funny way of showing it."

"Do I act like I love you... very much?"

I just nodded through my tears, and he pulled me closer. At this point, there were no more words.

The alarm rang far too early the following morning. I had to get up and get ready for work, and he had to pack his things and go. He got up and made us tea and biscuits with Nutella for breakfast and insisted on feeding me as tears ran down both of our faces. I left the apartment three times that morning, each time forgetting something I needed: keys, book bag, wallet. Each time I dreaded saying good-bye again, but not nearly as much as I dreaded leaving him. He had said that he would come back if he could, but we both knew that he would only be able to come back to me if he failed.

CHAPTER FORTY-FOUR

Grieving for Two

Soon after Ahmed left, I made my way back to the hospital to see my neurosurgeon. I needed to find out if I was pregnant and, if so, how my back surgery would affect things. He sent me to another doctor for a pregnancy test and a general checkup.

When I returned to my favorite doctor, he smiled at me.

"You're not pregnant, but you can try again."

I attempted to return his smile and nodded, thanking him for his time and promising to be there for my next checkup. He didn't know that Ahmed had left, and apparently, he didn't know what the other doctor had told me.

I was grieving the loss of not one, but two dreams that were close to my heart: the dream of a future with Ahmed and the dream of one day having a child.

Even though I was still fairly young, my body was shutting down. Chances are, there will be no children in my future, at least not of my own flesh and blood.

I always thought I had time. While others were building

relationships and futures, I spent a good part of my adult life traveling and learning about different places, cultures, and people. But I always thought I would have time to settle down one day and have that family.

I don't regret it... I would do it over just the same. Still, it was a high price to pay.

CHAPTER FORTY-FIVE

After the Rain

I don't know how I got through that day of teaching, or the next. At some point, I saw a picture that one of his friends added to his Facebook timeline. I knew that he would hate that picture, with his swollen, red eyes and forlorn expression as he sat on the floor packing his things. I figured his friend was going to hear about it, but I had gotten the message. (Not that I needed it.) Ahmed was hurting as much as I was.

We talked over Skype while he was staying with his friend in Costa Rica. Unfortunately, he wasn't able to visit any of the tourist sights that I've longed to see there, but he did send me a few pictures from a day out with his friend in their small town.

After about a month, he purchased a plane ticket to the Middle East with a layover in Europe. The idea was to find a way to remain in Europe while the second plane flew out without him. They allowed him to buy the ticket and pass through security, but he was turned away at the gate. Apparently, they had closed one of the loopholes that had allowed refugees to find a new place in the world.

He tried the same plan with various destinations, but never got past the check-out process. Then there was silence.

A few days later, I got a call. He had learned of a trick and was now safely in Europe, waiting to bring the rest of his family to join him. Now he needed to apply for refugee status, get a job, and find a home for them. He hesitated, and then his voice broke as he told me that he had planned to make that attempt his last; his final destination for that ticket had been Istanbul. He felt that he had done all that he could to fulfill his family's wishes and his responsibility as the oldest son. He had been on his way back to me. But on the last try, the plan worked. Success never tasted so bitter.

Even though he's in Europe, he might as well be a world away. I could have visited him, but he was confined to his uncle's home. He was quietly waiting for his application for refugee status to be accepted and to start the process of building a new life. He was far from the happy tourist that I would be. He had returned to the bosom of his family and community, and there was no place there for me.

We stayed in touch for a while, but "I miss you" starts to sound hollow after a while, even when it's true.

It's difficult to move on from a relationship without the fuel of anger to push me forward into a new life, but it's impossible for me to be angry with Ahmed.

It's true that he didn't put 'us' first, but his family needed him. If he hadn't done what he could to ensure their future happiness, he wouldn't have been the man I knew and loved.

And so I'm left with memories that make me smile much more often than they make me cry, and the knowledge that the kind of love I'm looking for is possible. He loved me unconditionally through one of the most challenging periods of my life, and in the process, he taught me how to love myself, flaws and all.

About the Author

Laureen Jordan was born in a small town in Northern California. She studied fine art and journalism as an undergraduate student. She later completed postgraduate studies in TESOL after spending a year studying abroad in Italy. Laureen spent much of her life teaching ESL, both in the US and abroad. She continues to teach, but also writes, creates artwork, and has a Reiki practice, Fair Winds Reiki & Mindfulness, in Reno, Nevada.

Laureen enjoys reading, traveling, dancing, and spending time with her family and friends.

Visit Laureen's website to join her reader list and receive an original short story about her first visit to Istanbul (which was referenced here in *On My Eye*). In the future, you will receive updates on upcoming novels and blog posts. You can unsubscribe at any time.

You can connect with me on:

- https://laureenjordan.com
- https://www.facebook.com/LaureenJordanAuthor
- https://mindfultravel.blog
- https://fairwindsreiki.com
- https://fairwindsreiki.wordpress.com

Subscribe to my newsletter:

- https://laureenjordan.com

Printed in Great Britain
by Amazon

43858548R00083